Date Due

NOV 7 1984			
NOV 10 1984			
NOV 21 1984			
DEC 6 1984			
MAR 5 1985			
MAR 12 1985			
APR 10 1985			
APR 30 1985			
JUL 17 1985			
NOV 30 [illegible]			
MAY 31 1994			

A Rose is a rose : a tribute to Pierre Elliott Trudeau in cartoons and quotes / introduction by Jack Macleod ; edited by Thad McIlroy. Toronto : Doubleday, 1984.

160 p. : ill.

"An Arcadia House book."

Text contains quotes by Trudeau.

Bibliography: p. 158.

(Continued on next card)

0385197888 pb 2267802
038519787X 2267810

A ROSE IS A ROSE

A ROSE IS A ROSE

A TRIBUTE TO
PIERRE ELLIOTT TRUDEAU
IN CARTOONS AND QUOTES

Introduction by
JACK MACLEOD

Edited by
THAD McILROY

AN ARCADIA HOUSE BOOK

DOUBLEDAY CANADA LIMITED, TORONTO, CANADA
DOUBLEDAY and COMPANY, INC., GARDEN CITY, NEW YORK
1984

AN ARCADIA HOUSE BOOK
Jack Jensen
Thad McIlroy
Garfield Reeves-Stevens

A Rose Is a Rose
A Tribute to Pierre Elliott Trudeau
in Cartoons and Quotes
Copyright © 1984 by Arcadia House Inc.
All rights reserved.

The copyright of the quotations and individual cartoons remains with their
originators or, in the case of the cartoonists, their respective newspaper affiliates.

CANADIAN CATALOGUING IN PUBLICATION DATA

A rose is a rose

Text contains quotes by Trudeau

ISBN 0-385-19788-8 (Bound) – – 0-385-19787-X (pbk.)

    1. Trudeau, Pierre Elliott, 1919-   - Cartoons, satire, etc.
    2. Canada - Politics and government - 1963-1984 - Caricatures and cartoons.
 *3. Canadian wit and humor, Pictorial.

 *I. Trudeau, Pierre Elliott, 1919-
 II. McIlroy, Thad, 1956-

FC626.T78R68 1984 971.064'4'0924 C84-098866-4
F1034.3.R68 1984

Special thanks to Nicholas Stahl/Miller Services, Peter Morris/Toronto Star
Syndicate, and David Persaud/Canada-Wide Feature Services for their kind help
in assembling the cartoons for this book.

Type generated from word-processing discs by
ALPHA GRAPHICS LIMITED
Printed and bound in Canada by
T.H. BEST PRINTING COMPANY, LTD.

DEDICATED TO

Pierre Elliott Trudeau

FOR BRINGING IT ALL BACK HOME

CONTENTS

9   FOREWORD

11   INTRODUCTION

13   THE BEGINNING

15   ELECTION '68

23   THE EARLY YEARS

41   PROVINCES AND PREMIERS

75   POLITICS

105   THE WORLD

129   THE CONSTITUTION

143   HERE TODAY
AND HERE TOMORROW

158   BIBLIOGRAPHY OF SOURCES

159   INDEX OF CARTOONISTS

160   A TEAR-STAINED REGRET

FOREWORD

A Rose Is a Rose is among the first books to appear marking the end of an era. It won't be the last. In fact, it's probably safe to predict that more books will be written about the past sixteen years than any other period in Canada's history. Most of these books, of course, will centre on the person who most influenced them, the person who most defined them: Pierre Elliott Trudeau.

It is also safe to predict that few of these books will agree in their depiction of Trudeau. Perhaps that is what attracted us most to him in 1968: he couldn't be pinned down or neatly labelled. But his mercurial nature certainly didn't stop some of us from trying. And those attempts are what make up this book.

From the almost unrecognizable early caricatures to the standard styles that we and the cartoonists grew comfortable with, here is Trudeau as seen through more than a dozen pairs of talented eyes. Not so surprisingly, what they saw is just what other Canadians saw, too.

Some Canadians loved Trudeau and some didn't. Some of us felt secret pleasure when he said exactly what he thought and others were shocked. This is how the cartoonists have portrayed him. A few of their depictions are warm, some not so warm, but all represent some part of what we all were thinking and feeling at the time. And all of them are funny.

This range of perceptions of Trudeau marks what may be a sign of the maturity of the Canadian voter: the fact that many people who did not like Trudeau's personal style (whatever that may be), and did not approve of his occasional bouts of forthright commentary, still gave him their confidence, and their votes.

In other words, no matter what they thought of Trudeau the person, they had faith in Trudeau the leader.

For a politician, for a Prime Minister, there is probably no higher honour. And there is probably no other world leader who deserves that honour more.

For all the differences in how the cartoonists portray Trudeau throughout this book, if you look carefully, you'll see that one element of most pictures never changes. It is a symbol of Trudeau; a little thing that added colour to the day; a sign of a particular unconventionality and a particular style.

What does it mean? Like most things, as much or as little as you want to make of it. We might look upon it as a symbol of the stability that Canada has enjoyed during a time of growing world unrest. Or we might see it as an indication that, like concern about unemployment and inflation, some things never change.

But for me, I'll just note that it is there and then leave it for the other books to analyse and interpret.

After all, a rose *is* a rose.

— *Thad McIlroy*

INTRODUCTION

The Trudeau years were the best of times; they were the worst of times. They were anything but dull. Now, our best cartoonists have given us laughing and lucid record of how it was.

These memorable cartoons capture the Trudeau era in a deft and imaginatively funny way. They also remind us of La Rochefoucauld's maxim that we always like those who admire us, but we do not always like those whom we admire. For some Canadians, admiration for Trudeau has been grudging. Sometimes he has seemed to treat us with disdain or contempt. Sometimes we have viewed him with a mixture of wonderment and loathing. He has exasperated us as much as he has intrigued us.

But then, politics is usually all about human frailty and paradox. Politics has been termed the noblest of callings and the vilest of practices. There has been no Canadian politician more paradoxical than our P.E.T. He has been a professor and a playboy, a millionaire who, in 1949, stood by the workers against the strike-breaking police of Duplessis, and a civil-libertarian lawyer who invoked the War Measures Act in October of 1970. He has been a politician who performed flips into swimming pools and somersaults on fundamental policy, as over wage and price controls. He has disported himself as a sophisticated European-style intellectual who also makes generous use of an up-thrust middle finger, a charmer who frequently antagonizes, and a statesman who sometimes seems to want to play public games of sillybuggers.

How are we ordinary hosers supposed to understand this complex, strutting contradiction of a man? With his dashing image, his mask-like face that Marshal McLuhan said was like an icon on TV, maybe the cartoonists capture him better than anyone else.

Like the celebrated Reversible Falls of New Brunswick, it's difficult to tell about Trudeau what is truth and what is illusion. But a few clever lines by accomplished cartoonists can briskly sketch him moving in either direction.

Anyone who remembers the euphoric "Trudeaumania" of 1968 will recall the rows and rows of liberal intellectuals and wild-eyed media gurus fairly drooling over this astonishing new presence, this potential political saviour. Was it possible that, after the petty ravings and sordid hassles of the Diefenbaker and Pearson years, we had actually elected an entirely fresh and different sort of leader? Perhaps even a "philosopher-king"? The final judgement will depend on the perspective of history.

The historian Ramsay Cook once wrote that Canada has produced only two political thinkers of any stature, George Grant and

Pierre Trudeau. Cook may exaggerate, yet he is not all wrong. The brilliant mental prowess of Trudeau has never been in doubt. On the other hand, just as Einstein was said to make errors in simple arithmetic, the best theorists sometimes are not solid practitioners and the best intellectuals may lack common sense as well as the common touch.

Trudeau was often not only tough but inspirational, reminding us of standards of excellence. He was demanding of Canadians, and demanding of himself. Without question, he succeeded where all others had failed in bringing home the Constitution, with the bonus of a Charter of Rights. He fought the good fight against Separatism and Rene Levesque's referendum. Because of Trudeau, bilingualism became a fact. In some ways he elevated the tone of our public life as well as burnishing Canada's profile abroad. As Prime Minister he had guts and flash. Above all, he displayed insouciant style and daring. He was "for real," and totally his own man.

But history may less prominently record that he also governed in the face of world economic decline, rocketing inflation, rising unemployment, and whalloping deficits. Many of his bold improvisations simply did not work, and when they didn't, his response was a jaunty "fuddle-duddle."

Thus, we have regarded him with frequent surprise and compelled admiration. He irritated us, he goaded us, but he never bored us. Maybe the inner truth of the man can be captured only by the superior but lengthy prose of a Richard Gwyn, or a Christina McCall . . . or by the nimble fingers of the snappy cartoonists.

Never underestimate the pleasure and the power to be found in political drawings. Like great baseball players, they make the difficult, even the impossible "catch," seem easy. A few economical lines on a white page, and there is a revealing glimpse of a truth. In recent years, Canadian political cartoonists have come of age and reached world-class standards. The best of them are to be found in these pages.

If the pundit's columns or the ponderous editorials are the broadswords of commentary, the cartoon is the stiletto. Although we tend to think in terms of fine art and minor art, really all creativity comes in only two categories, good and bad, and our political cartoonists are superb. There's something unforgettable and magic about a biting cartoon. The simple but eloquent drawing presents the *Haiku* of personalities and politics; minimal presentation, but maximum impact.

Plain and unassuming, yet incisive, each cartoon is a visual epigram and each artist has a unique style and stamp. The best political cartoonists are like the best political leaders: they do not echo or remind you of anyone else. Such talents are to be treasured.

And so we come back, inexorably, to the figure who dominates this book, the leader who never reminded you of anyone else, Pierre Elliott Trudeau. You have your own opinion of this remarkable man, this elusive image . . . what can I tell you? Let's leave it to the Bard:

> "... the elements
> So mixed in him that Nature might stand up
> And say to all the world, 'This was a man.'"

Or further:

> "He was a man, take him for all in all,
> [We] shall not look on his like again."

— *Jack Macleod*

(Jack Macleod teaches unscientific political science at the University of Toronto and is the author of the novels *Zinger and Me* and *Going Grand*.)

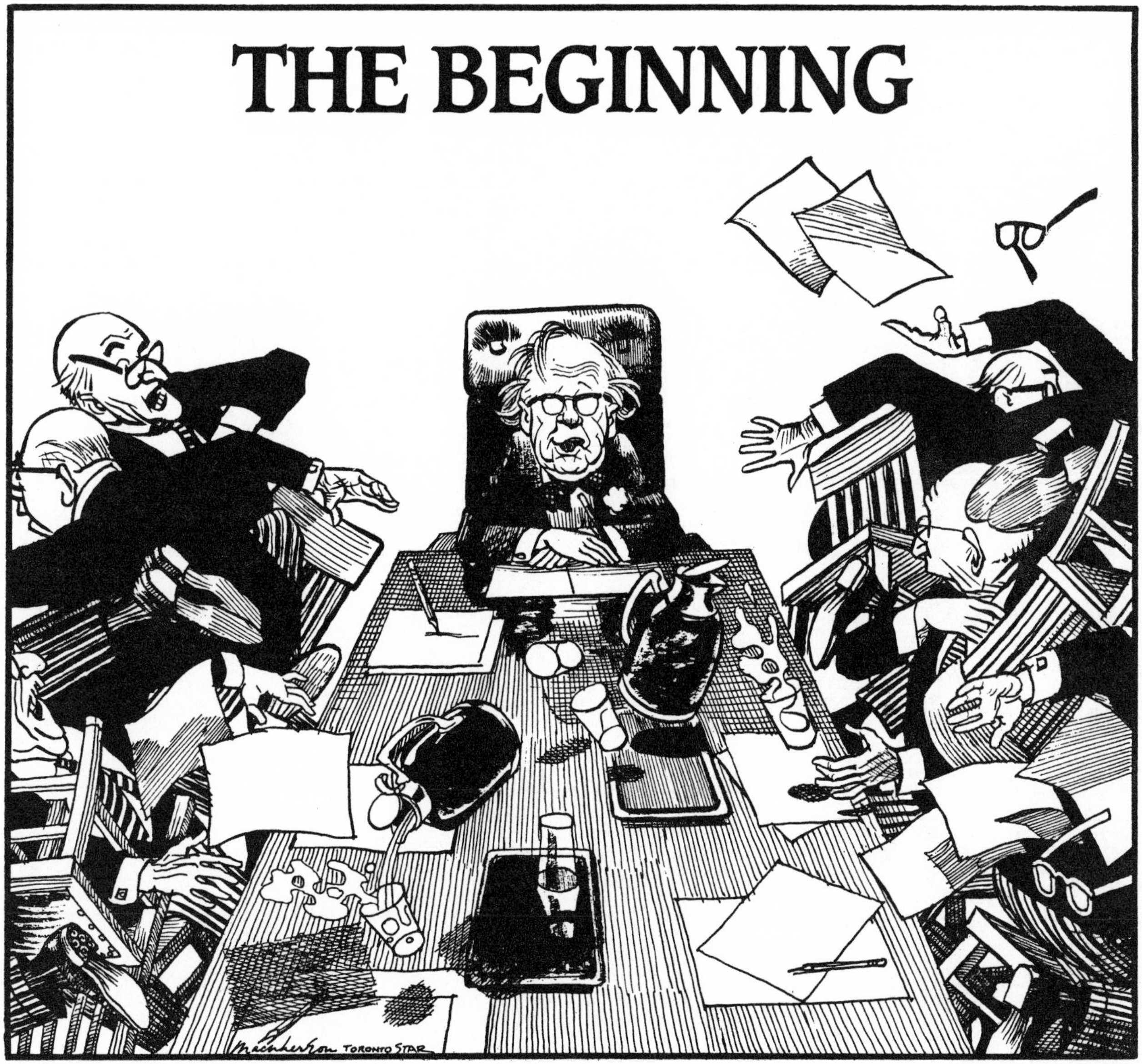
THE BEGINNING
Macpherson TORONTO STAR

DUNCAN MACPHERSON
THE TORONTO STAR, MARCH 9, 1966

"Any volunteers for Minister of Justice?"

"So I went to see Mr. Pearson and I said, 'Here are three good men (Marchand, Trudeau, and Pelletier) who want to join the party and there is some hesitation from (Guy) Favreau.' 'Well,' he said, 'I'll speak to Favreau.'"
—Maurice Sauve describing the recruitment of
Trudeau to the Liberal Party,
July-September, 1965
from Lester Pearson and the Dream of Unity
by Peter Stursberg

"Trudeau turned out, rather to his own surprise, to be an extremely effective campaigner, at least in the white-collar riding of Mount Royal. A born teacher, he thoroughly enjoyed the give-and-take of political meetings, especially the all-candidates debates popular in suburban Mount Royal. His wry humour went down well."
—Blair Fraser
Maclean's, *January 22, 1966*

"It was that televised constitutional conference in early February, 1968, that made a relatively new Member of Parliament and the recently appointed Justice Minister, Pierre Elliott Trudeau, a national figure. It could be said that John Roberts and his Confederation of Tomorrow Conference were responsible for Trudeau's becoming Liberal Leader and Prime Minister, to which Robarts replied, 'The Lord works in mysterious ways His wonders to perform.'"
—Peter Stursberg
Lester Pearson and the Dream of Unity

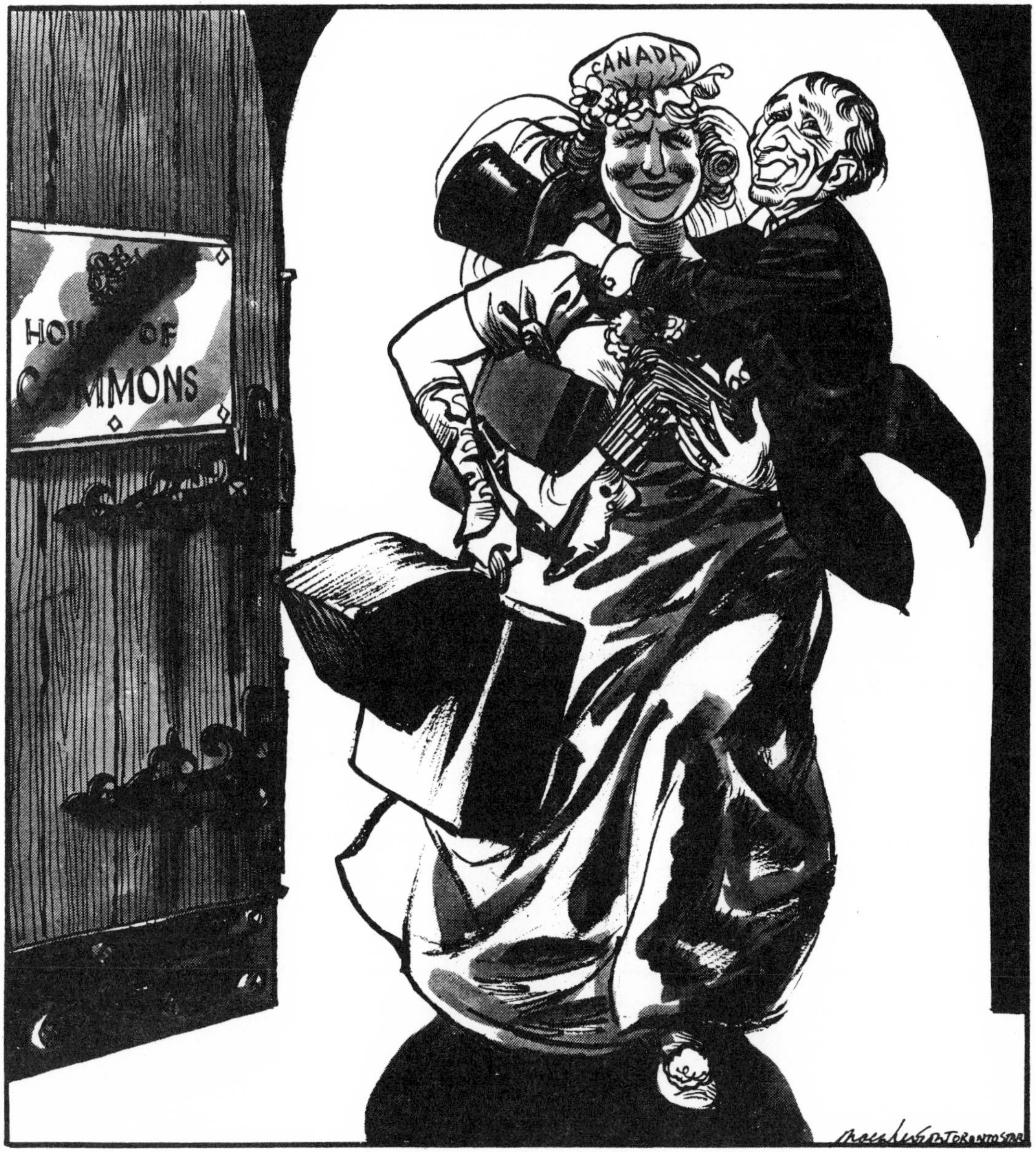
CANADA
HOUSE OF
COMMONS

DUNCAN MACPHERSON
THE TORONTO STAR, SEPTEMBER 12, 1968

ELECTION '68

"The Trudeau campaign completely bewildered the old pros like Paul Martin, who could not understand the secret of its success. As Paul said to me: 'How can someone who knows nothing of politics or the party get so much support so suddenly, even from people like Joe Smallwood?' The answer was simple. Canadians thought of Paul Martin, or even of Paul Hellyer, in the context of Mackenzie King. They thought of Pierre Trudeau as a man for this season, uncontaminated and uninhibited."

—Lester B. Pearson
in Mike: The Memoirs of the
Right Honourable Lester B. Pearson

"They follow him about as though they suspect he has some trick they might master."

"If you look closely at Trudeau's eyes, you realize he is about as casual as a computer."

—Peter C. Newman
commenting on the 1968 convention
in Home Country

"Trudeau said no up to the end... I said to Pierre, 'In this business this is an opportunity. If you miss it, you don't know when it's going to come back...'

"... Finally, he said, 'Well, okay, let's try'..."
—Jean Marchand describing Trudeau's decision
to run for the Liberal leadership in
February, 1968 from Lester Pearson
and the Dream of Unity
by Peter Stursberg

"To Trudeau and his fellow Idea-men, the Canadian political scene had far too long been the exclusive preserve of the sentimentalists and the necromancers. Instead of National Dreaming there would now be a firm grip on reality; instead of crystal balls— real balls."

—Larry Zolf
The Dance of the Dialectic

DUNCAN MACPHERSON
THE TORONTO STAR, APRIL, 1968

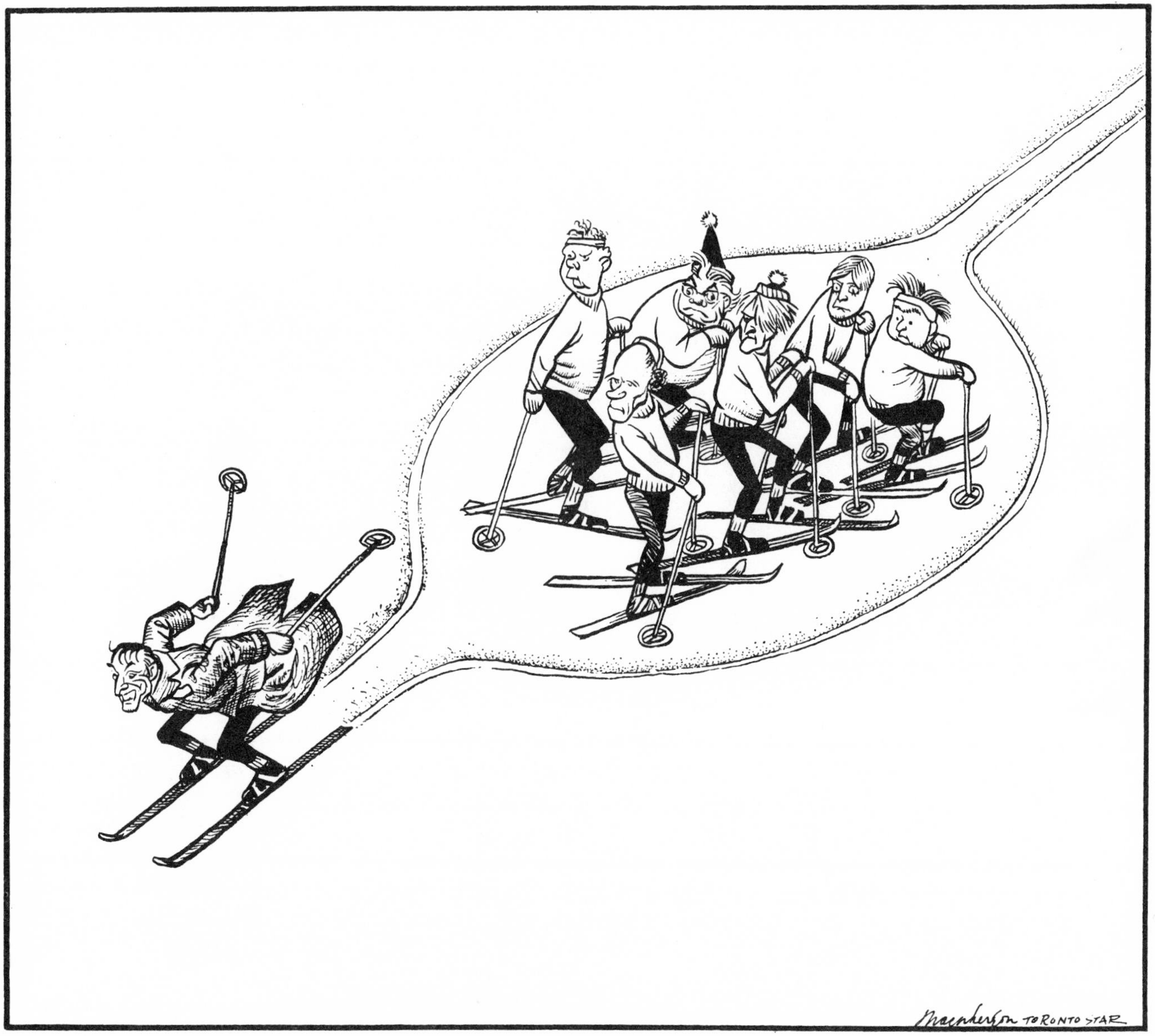
Macpherson TORONTO STAR

"The main interest centres on Mr. Trudeau, a colorful, freethinking intellectual whose taste for sandals, bright shirts and casual ascots will bring a new look to the Justice Department...

"Mr. Pearson quipped yesterday that people knew Mr. Trudeau was going to be appointed to the Cabinet because he showed up in the House wearing a tie."

—Anthony Westell, The Globe and Mail
April 5, 1967

"(After meeting Trudeau for the first time [February, 1968]) I said, 'This man is an outstanding man in the world today. He's got ability and talent that's on a world scale. Myself, I feel like a clumsy elephant with arthritis.' That went all across Canada.

"I said, 'Gentlemen, you've just met the next Prime Minister of Canada,' and I came out for Trudeau."

—Joey Smallwood
from Lester Pearson and the Dream of Unity
by Peter Stursberg

FRANKLIN
THE GLOBE AND MAIL, APRIL 24, 1968

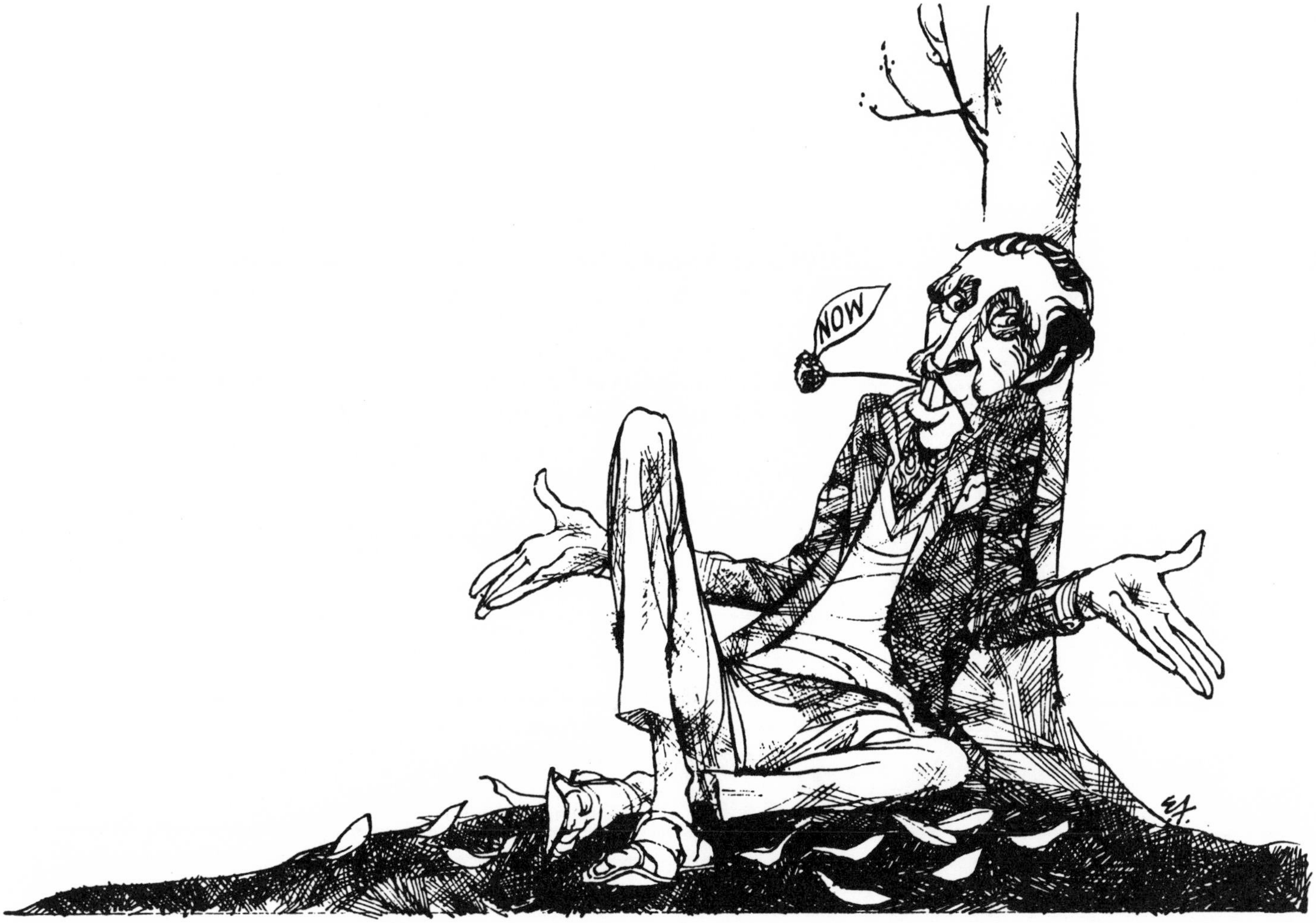
NOW

"Before a thousand newspaper stories had declared him a glamorous bachelor, and a hundred television cameras had worked their peculiar magic on the sharp planes of his unusual face, he was noteworthy mainly to those who recognized the quality of his mind. If the political pros in the Liberal Party in either the old or the new guard had been told at any time during his first eighteen months in Parliament that he was leadership material they would have roared with derision."

—*Christina McCall Newman*
Grits

"Trudeaumania! An unexplained phenomenon believed to be related to the virus that causes lemming to rush into the sea."

—*Charles Lynch*
Southam News Services

"The leadership campaign was a joy; we (the press) revelled in it. We dashed around the country asking people whom *they* would back for the Liberal leadership, and if they weren't sure, we told them... On the daily papers, Trudeau-watchers blossomed; as the campaign wore on, his step became springier, his wit wittier, his smile more glowing, his athletic prowess more dazzling. That wasn't him, it was us. He was good copy, and we made him better."

—*Walter Stewart*
Shrug: Trudeau in Power

"Have you ever seen him kiss a farmer?"

—*John G. Diefenbaker*
Columbo's Canadian Quotations

"If it puckers, he's there."

—*Walter Stewart*
Shrug: Trudeau in Power

REIDFORD
THE GLOBE AND MAIL

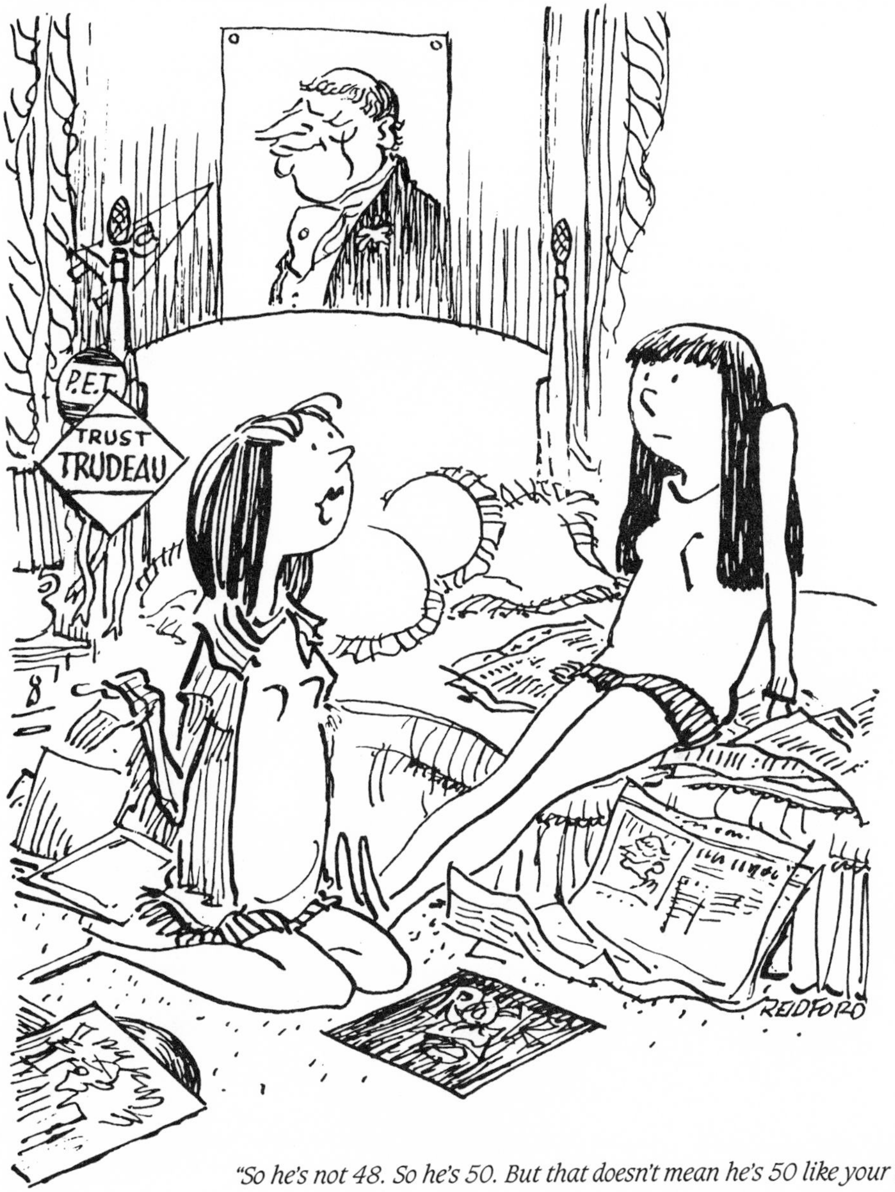
P.E.T.
TRUST TRUDEAU
REIDFORD

"So he's not 48. So he's 50. But that doesn't mean he's 50 like your father!"

THE EARLY YEARS

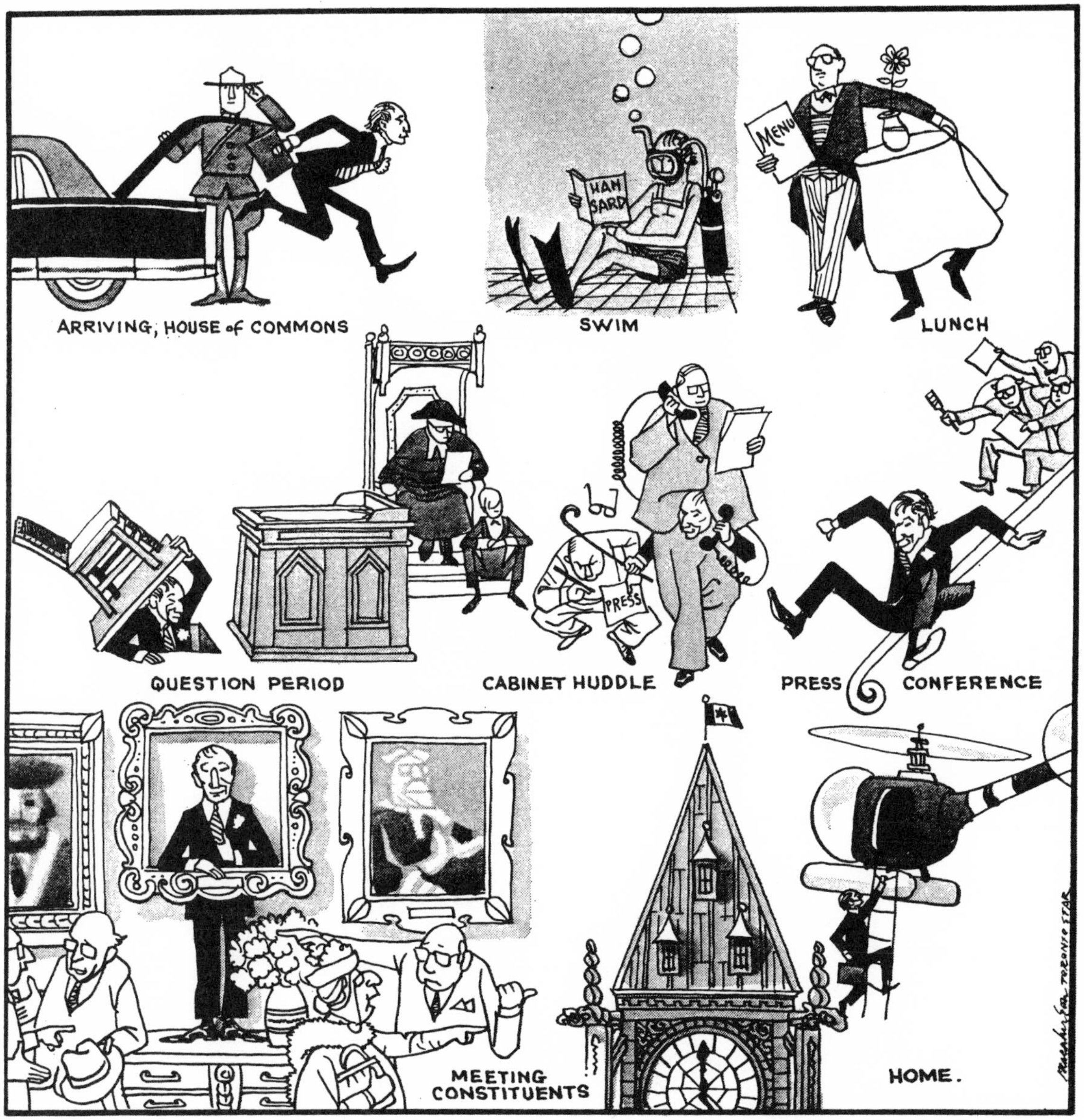
ARRIVING, HOUSE of COMMONS
HAM SARD
SWIM
MENU
LUNCH
QUESTION PERIOD
PRESS
CABINET HUDDLE
PRESS CONFERENCE
MEETING CONSTITUENTS
HOME.

The Secret Life of Pierre Elliott Trudeau.

DUNCAN MACPHERSON
THE TORONTO STAR, MAY 22, 1969

"**Of course, a** bilingual state is more expensive than a unilingual one, but it is a richer state."
—*Pierre Elliott Trudeau*
April, 1968

"**It is possible** to be, at one and the same time, a good Canadian and a good Quebecker."
—*Pierre Elliott Trudeau, Television address*
November 24, 1977

DUNCAN MACPHERSON
THE TORONTO STAR, MAY 22, 1968

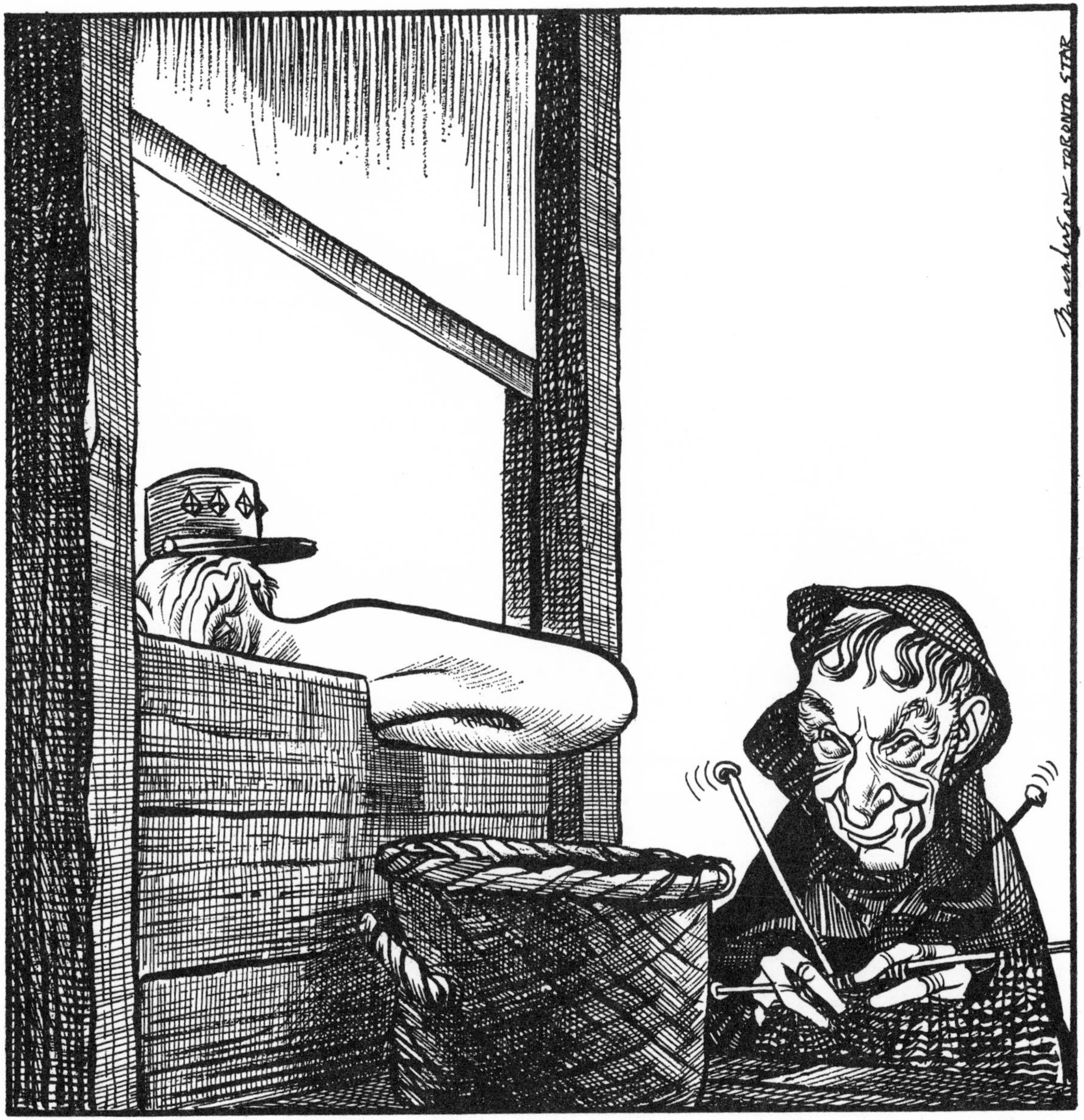
TORONTO STAR

Vive Le Quebec Libre

"The attainment of a just society is the
cherished hope of civilized men."
—Speech from the Throne, House of Commons
September 12, 1968

"Mr. Trudeau was a Hegelian; in 1968, as the
new Prime Minister, more anointed than
elected by the Canadian people, Mr. Trudeau
was a philosopher king."
—Larry Zolf

"We are like the pilots of a supersonic
aeroplane. By the time an airport comes into
the pilot's field of vision, it is too late to begin
the landing procedure. Such planes must be
navigated by radar. A political party, in
formulating policy, can act as society's radar."
—Pierre Elliott Trudeau, November 1969
Liberal Party Thinkers' Conference

"If we could only all be saints we could have
this perfect society. But we ain't."
—Pierre Elliott Trudeau, 1969
from Home Country *by Peter C. Newman*

"This is an exciting country; one which offers
to every man and woman the hope and
promise of a better tomorrow. Dreaming and
planning are part of the Canadian character. I
hope they will always be."
—Pierre Elliott Trudeau
February, 1971

REIDFORD
THE GLOBE AND MAIL, APRIL 27, 1972

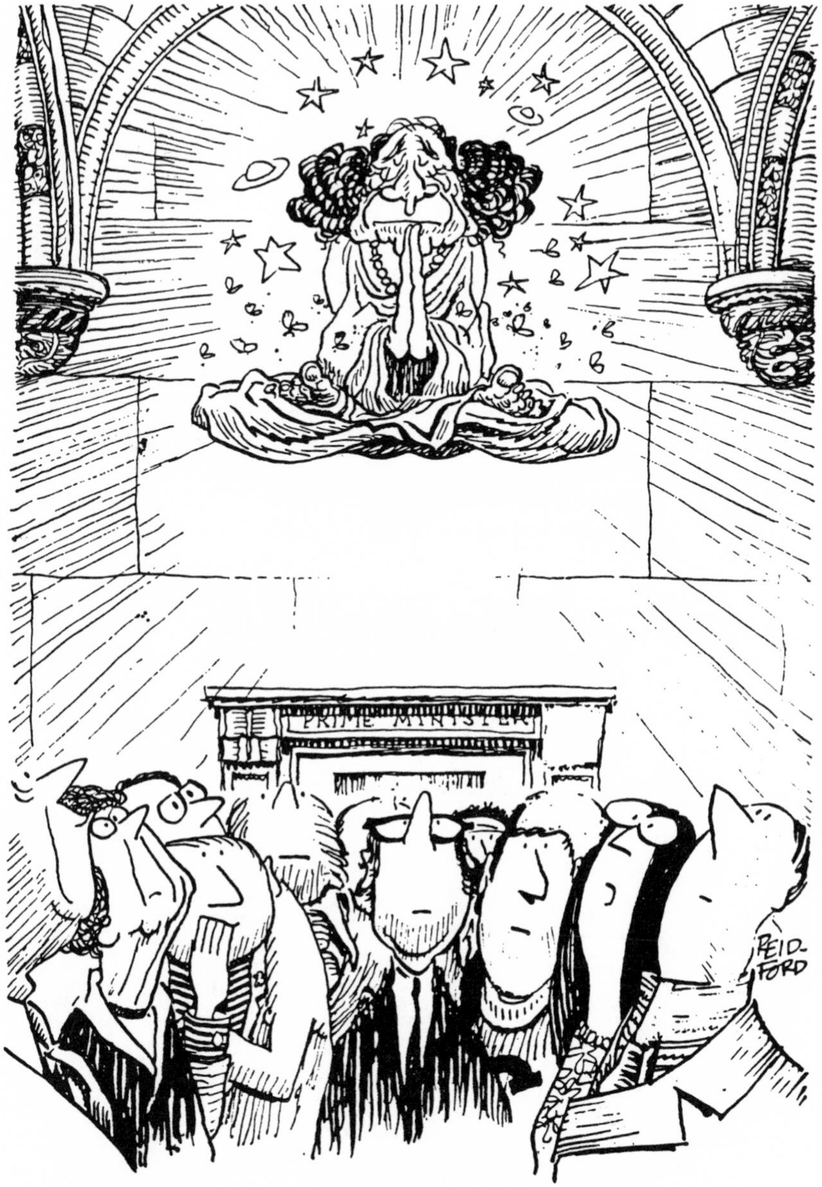
PRIME MINISTER
REIDFORD

"There he goes again!"

"These are strong powers (The War Measures Act) and I find them as distasteful as I'm sure you do. They are necessary, however, to permit the police to deal with persons who advocate or promote the violent overthrow of the democratic system."
—Pierre Elliott Trudeau
October 16, 1970
from Rumours of War *by Ron Haggart and*
Aubrey E. Golden

"...when he said, 'I am speaking to you at a moment of grave crisis,' (it) made a wonderfully dramatic impact. It is, in fact, impossible to substitute the figure of any preceding Canadian Prime Minister in the role of Pierre Trudeau during the October Crisis."
—Doris French Shackleton
in Tommy Douglas

"Trudeau is the last man in this country to panic. We moved because it was that or chaos in the Government of Quebec and among the people."
—Douglas Fisher, quoting a 'top level source'
in The Toronto Telegram, *October, 1970*
from Rumours of War *by Ron Haggart and*
Aubrey E. Golden

DUNCAN MACPHERSON
THE TORONTO STAR, OCTOBER 20, 1970

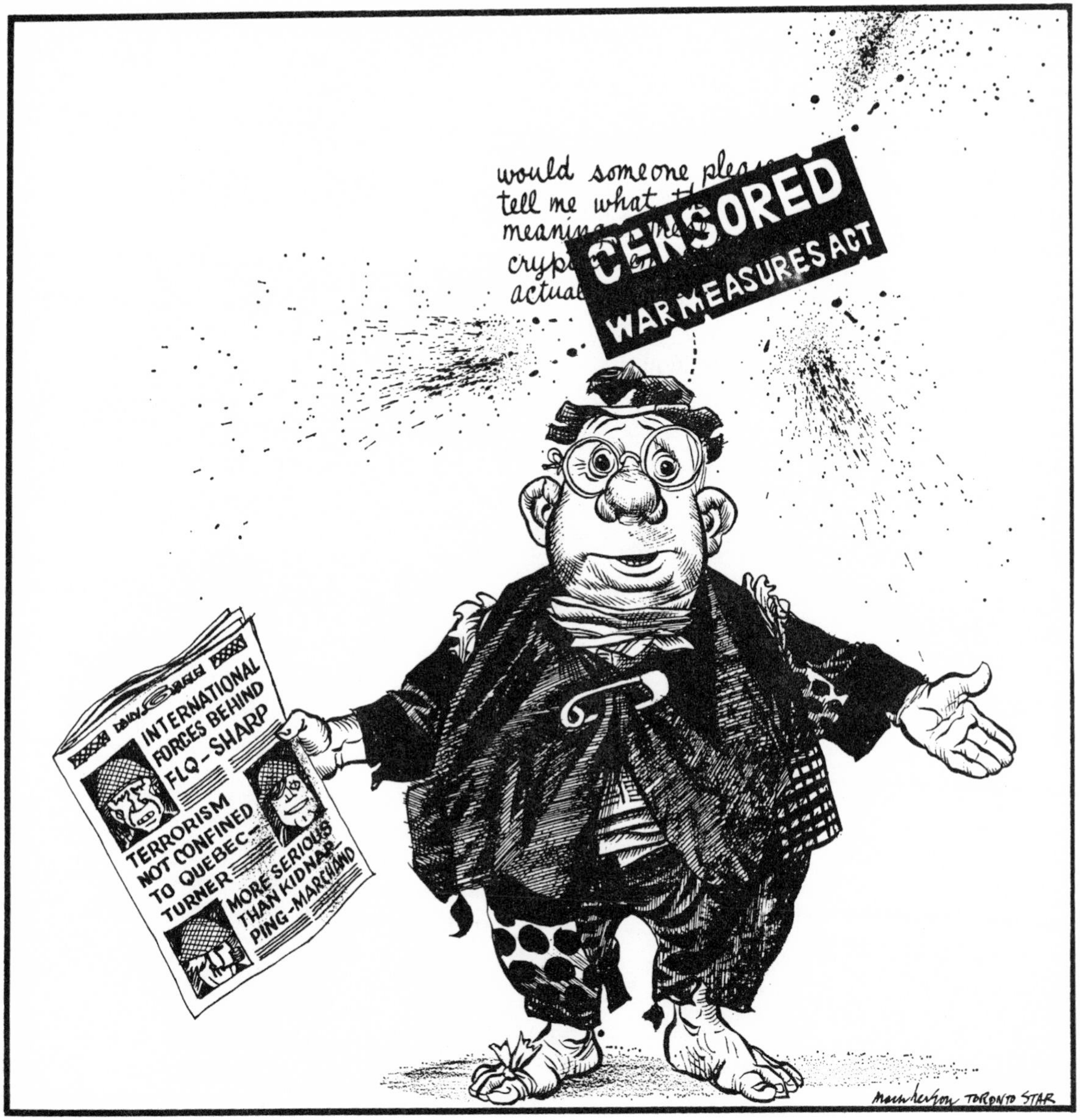
would someone plea
tell me what
meanin
cryp
actual
CENSORED
WAR MEASURES ACT
INTERNATIONAL FORCES BEHIND FLQ - SHARP
TERRORISM NOT CONFINED TO QUEBEC - TURNER
MORE SERIOUS THAN KIDNAP - PING-MARCHAND
Macpherson TORONTO STAR

"Fuddle duddle."

—Pierre Elliott Trudeau
February 16, 1971

DUNCAN MACPHERSON
THE TORONTO STAR, FEBRUARY 19, 1971

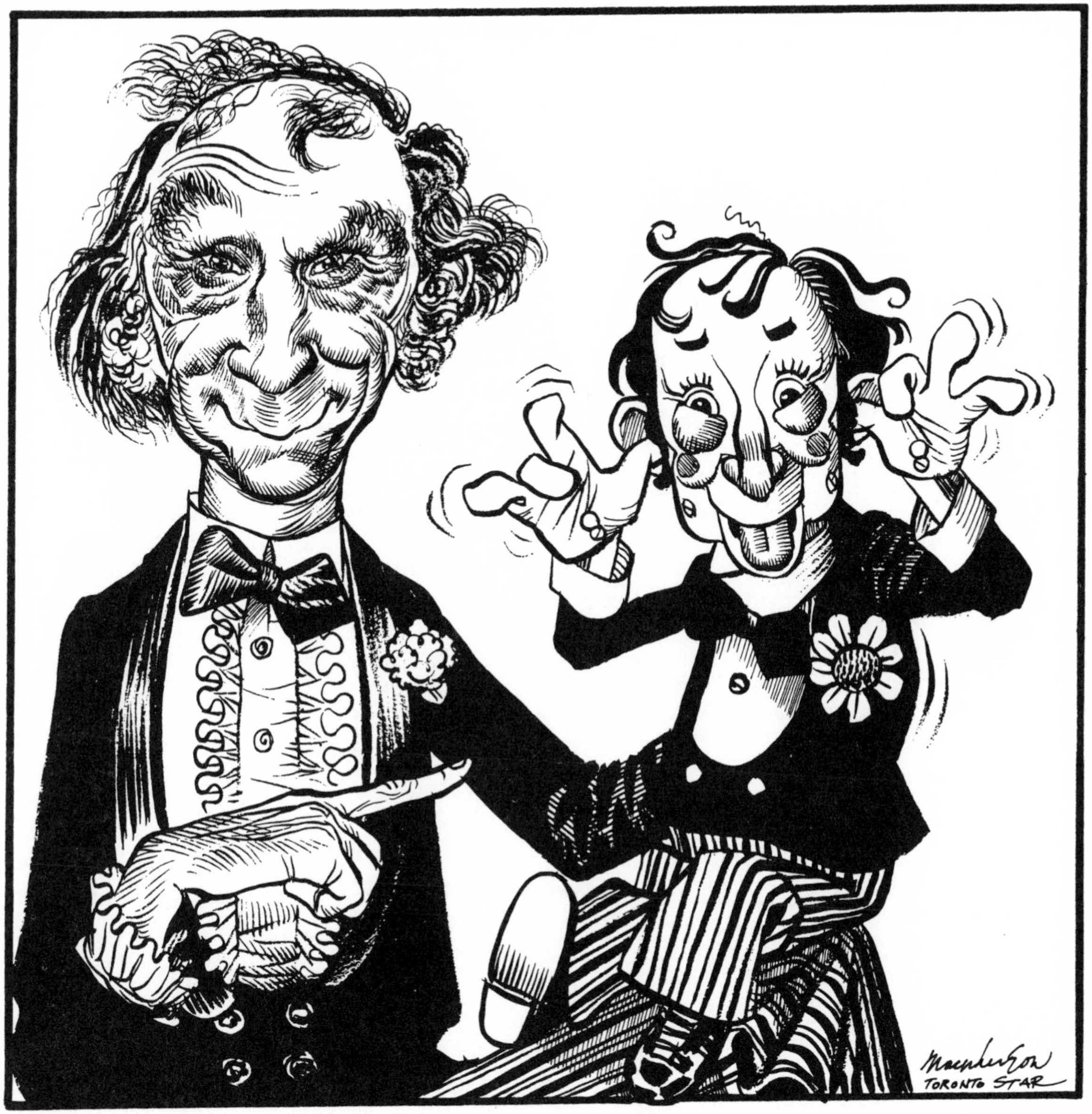
Macpherson
TORONTO STAR

"He had come into politics from outside the Liberal Party and had had no experience with the internal dynamic of such a motley, changeable group of volunteers. But if the 1972 election results were a warning that Trudeau did not know his own party, the 1974 election campaign was to show that this political amateur was able to learn new skills."
—*Stephen Clarkson*
"Pierre Trudeau and the Liberal Party:
The Jockey and the Horse"
in Canada at the Polls:
The General Election of 1974
Howerd R. Penniman (ed.)

"The more the loss was discussed by Trudeau's friends, opponents, intimates and critics, the more apparent it became that the election result was due to one central fact: Trudeau had committed the cardinal sin for a politician, he had lost touch with his constituency."
—*Peter C. Newman commenting on the 1972*
election
in Home Country

"The land is Strong."
—*1972 Liberal Campaign Slogan*

DUNCAN MACPHERSON
THE TORONTO STAR, SEPTEMBER 19, 1972

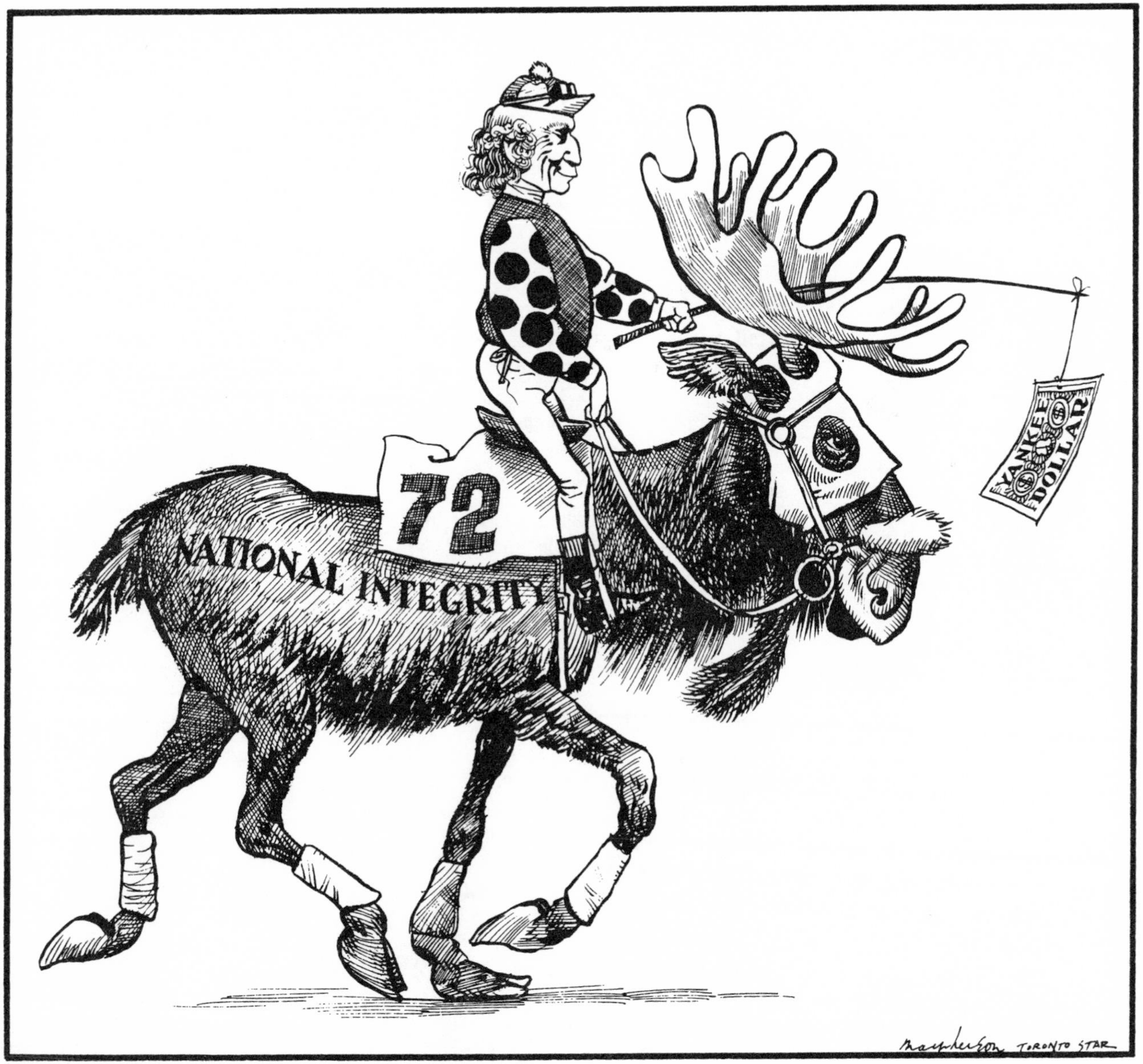
72
NATIONAL INTEGRITY
YANKEE DOLLAR
Macpherson TORONTO STAR

Election Stakes: Weather cloudy; track slow; foreign ownership (scratched); Best Bet: Corporate Bum (Lewis).

"I'll tell you one thing that's certain. From now on, no more philosopher-king."
—Pierre Elliott Trudeau
Columbo's Canadian Quotations

"I see a campaign as a bath of fire in which you're purified and settle all the piddling little questions of whether this little thing was right or wrong. What's your over-all judgement? Is it yes or no?"
—Pierre Elliott Trudeau
September 2, 1972

"We got an awful shellacking from the Canadian people."
—Pierre Elliott Trudeau commenting on the
1972 election December, 1982

"(The New Democrats) are hanging onto us like seagulls on a fishing vessel, claiming that they are really steering the ship."
—Pierre Elliott Trudeau
March, 1974 (Minority Government)

"The Romans used to say *'vox populi, vox Dei'* (the voice of the people is the voice of God) and in some ways the people are always right.
"And for we politicians, particularly when we see good people go down around us we have to say that the people are right, but the ways of people and the ways of God are sometimes devious and difficult to understand."
—Pierre Elliott Trudeau
April, 1979

MERLE TINGLEY
LONDON FREE PRESS, 1973

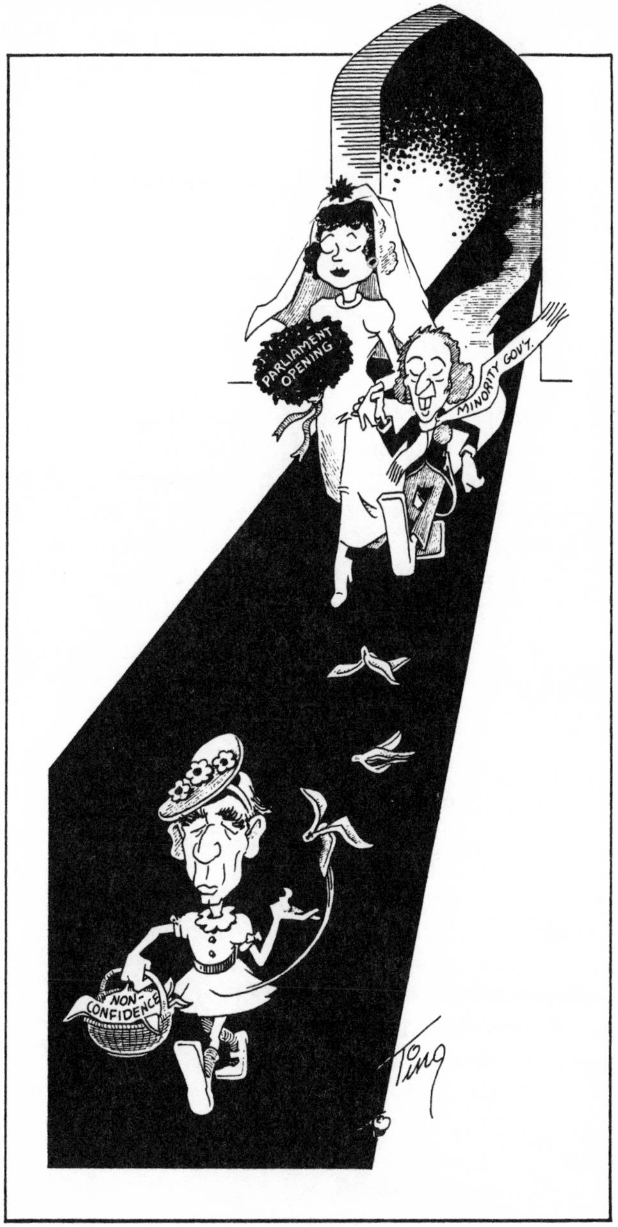
PARLIAMENT OPENING
MINORITY GOV'T.
NON-CONFIDENCE
Ting

"After asking him to take on the (campaign co-chairman) job [in Spring, 1973], Trudeau said politely he hoped he wasn't interrupting (Keith) Davey's dinner. Davey told him he was watching hockey and added that the Buffalo Sabres were winning the game. There was an awkward pause at the other end of the line and then Trudeau said, 'Oh, I see. What inning are they in?'"

—Christina McCall Newman
Grits

"In this (1974) campaign (Keith) Davey said, 'When I tell the Prime Minister to shine his shoes, he shines his shoes.'

"Shoes gleaming, his lovely young bride at his side— smiling demurely and remarking that Pierre had 'taught me all I know about love'— Trudeau waltzed through a happy campaign. He was a politician now, transformed, as Larry Zolf remarked, from a philosopher-king to Mackenzie King."

—Val Sears
in Farewell to the 70s

"...One of these guys said, 'I have a friend, Mr. Prime Minister, a kid who lives in Scarborough, who wants very much to buy a house and he just can't afford to, the prices are so terribly high. What will I say to him?' And I remember the Prime Minister saying: 'Tell him to move to Regina.' And it was just— God, it was just awful."

—Keith Davey recalling
a meeting between Trudeau
and Toronto Liberal organizers at the start
of the 1974 campaign

FRANKLIN
THE GLOBE AND MAIL, AUGUST 3, 1973

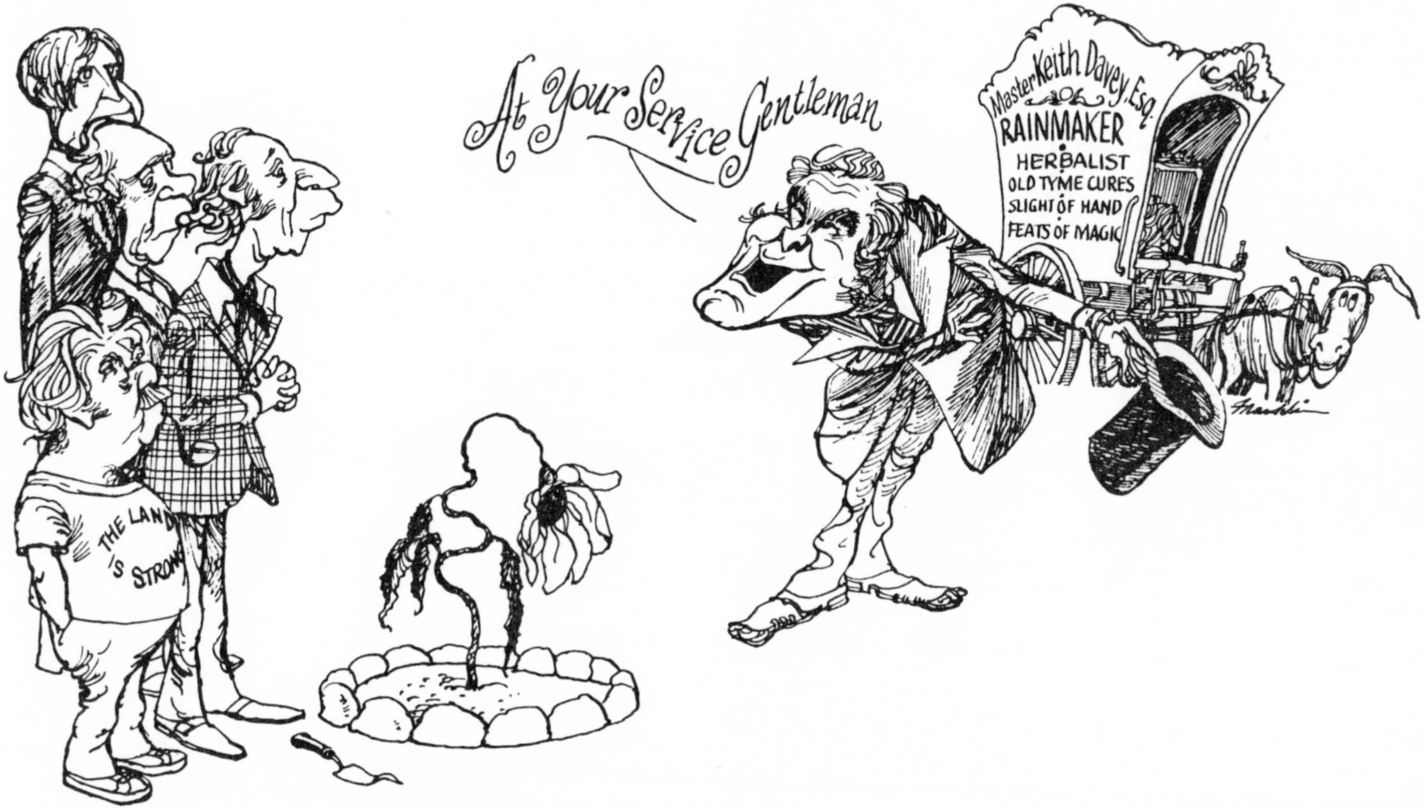
At Your Service Gentleman
Master Keith Davey, Esq.
RAINMAKER
HERBALIST
OLD TYME CURES
SLIGHT OF HAND
FEATS OF MAGIC
THE LAND 'S STRONG

"Zap, you're frozen."
—Pierre Elliott Trudeau commenting on
Robert Stanfield's proposal for wage and price
controls
June 29, 1974

"We have to swallow strong medicine... We
need to cool the fires of inflation."
—Pierre Elliott Trudeau announcing wage and
price controls
October 13, 1975

FRANKLIN
THE GLOBE AND MAIL, JULY 1, 1974

"How about promising two Dominion Days?"

PROVINCES AND PREMIERS

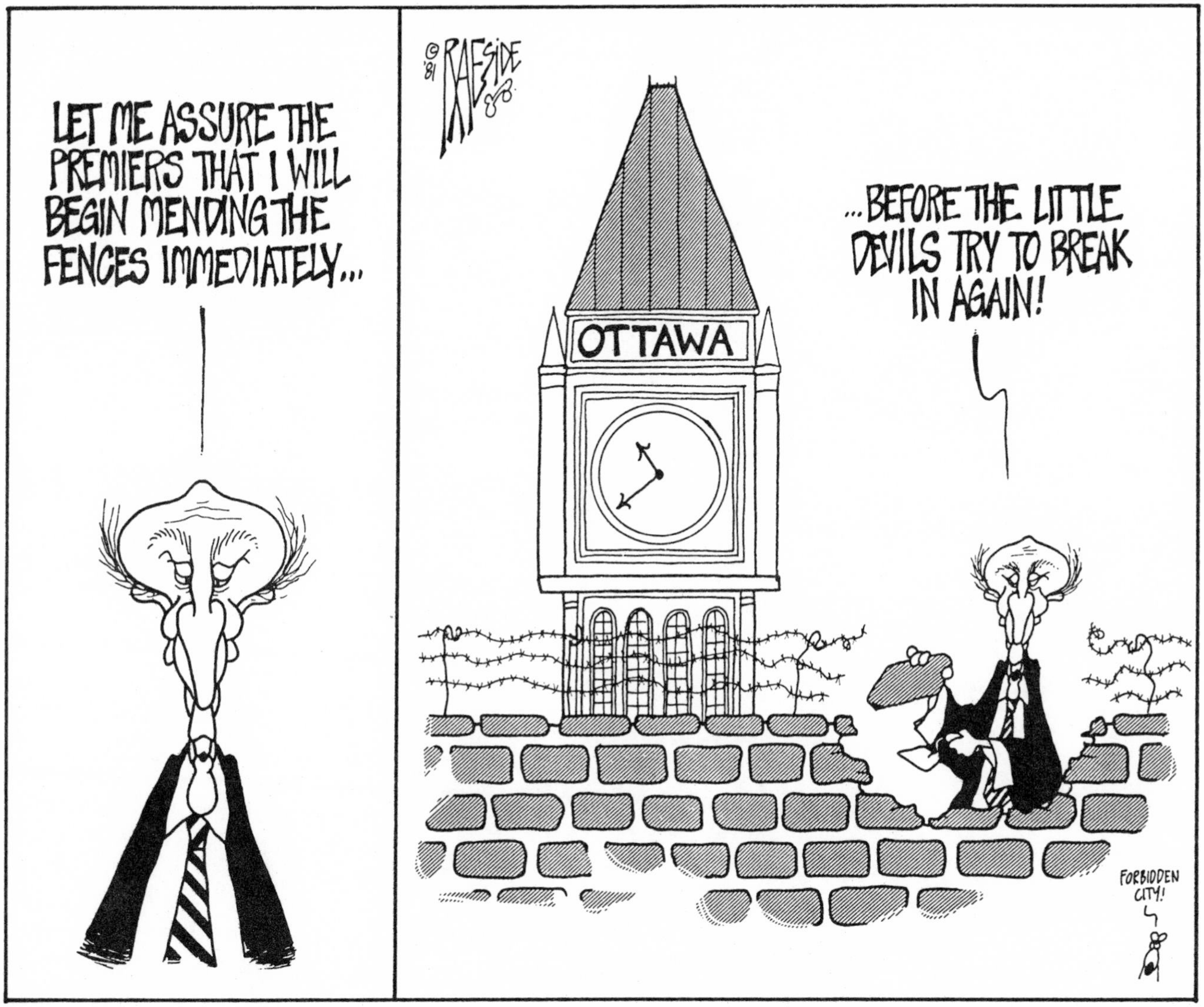
LET ME ASSURE THE PREMIERS THAT I WILL BEGIN MENDING THE FENCES IMMEDIATELY...
OTTAWA
...BEFORE THE LITTLE DEVILS TRY TO BREAK IN AGAIN!
FORBIDDEN CITY!

ADRIAN RAESIDE
TIMES-COLONIST

"There is a deeper bond than that of blood.
There is the bond of fraternity, for if Canada is
to survive it can only survive in mutual respect
and in love of one another."
—Pierre Elliott Trudeau
November 26, 1976

REIDFORD
THE GLOBE AND MAIL, DECEMBER 8, 1969

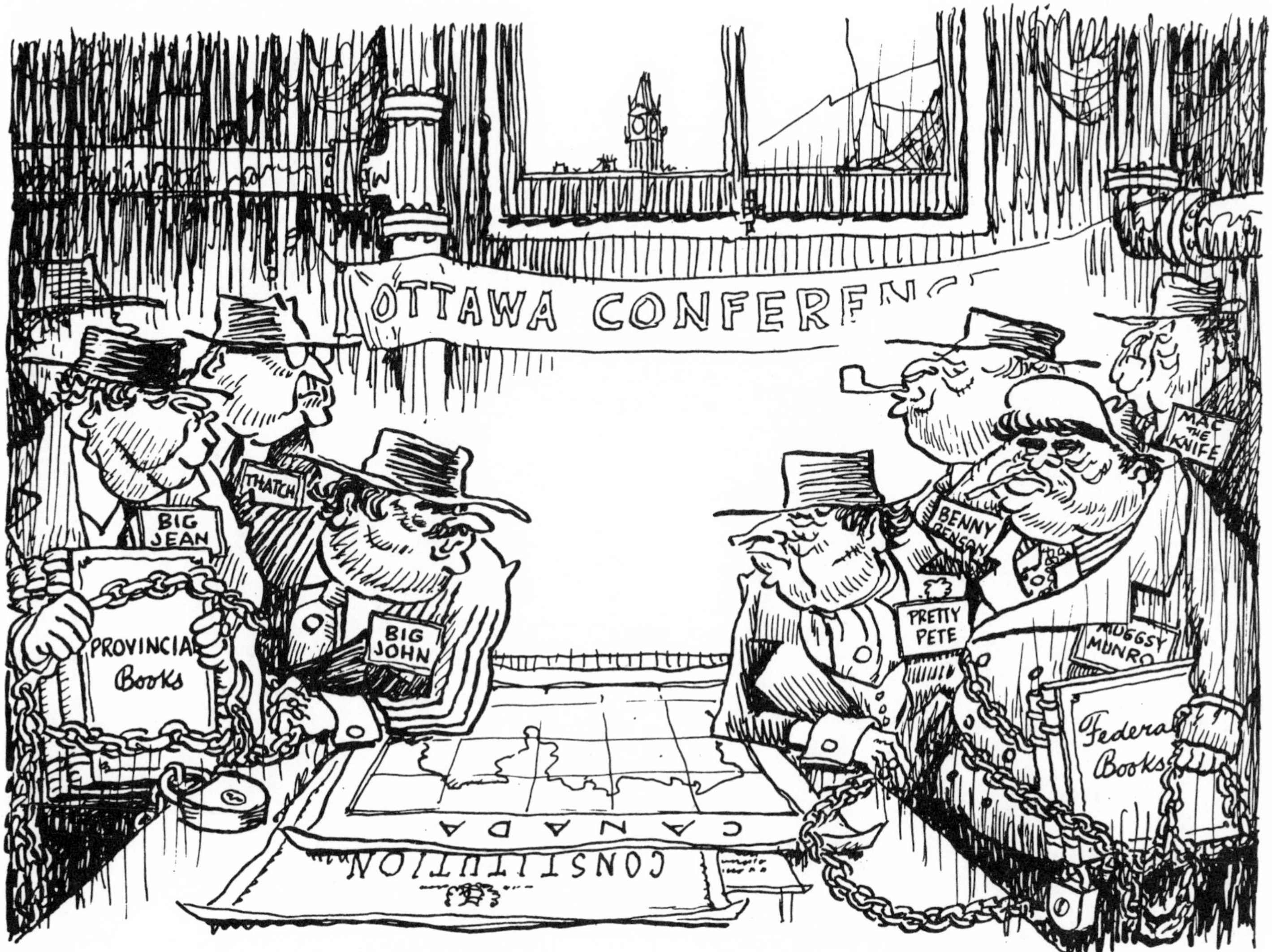
OTTAWA CONFERE
THATCH
BIG JEAN
PROVINCIA Books
BIG JOHN
BENNY
PRETTY PETE
MAC THE KNIFE
MUNRO
Federa Books
CANADA
CONSTITUTION

"So yuz wanna move into health insurance, Pretty Pierre?"

"The role of government policy should not be
to direct and manage the economy in detail."
—*Speech from the Throne, 1976*

*BLAINE
THE HAMILTON SPECTATOR, MAY 8, 1981*

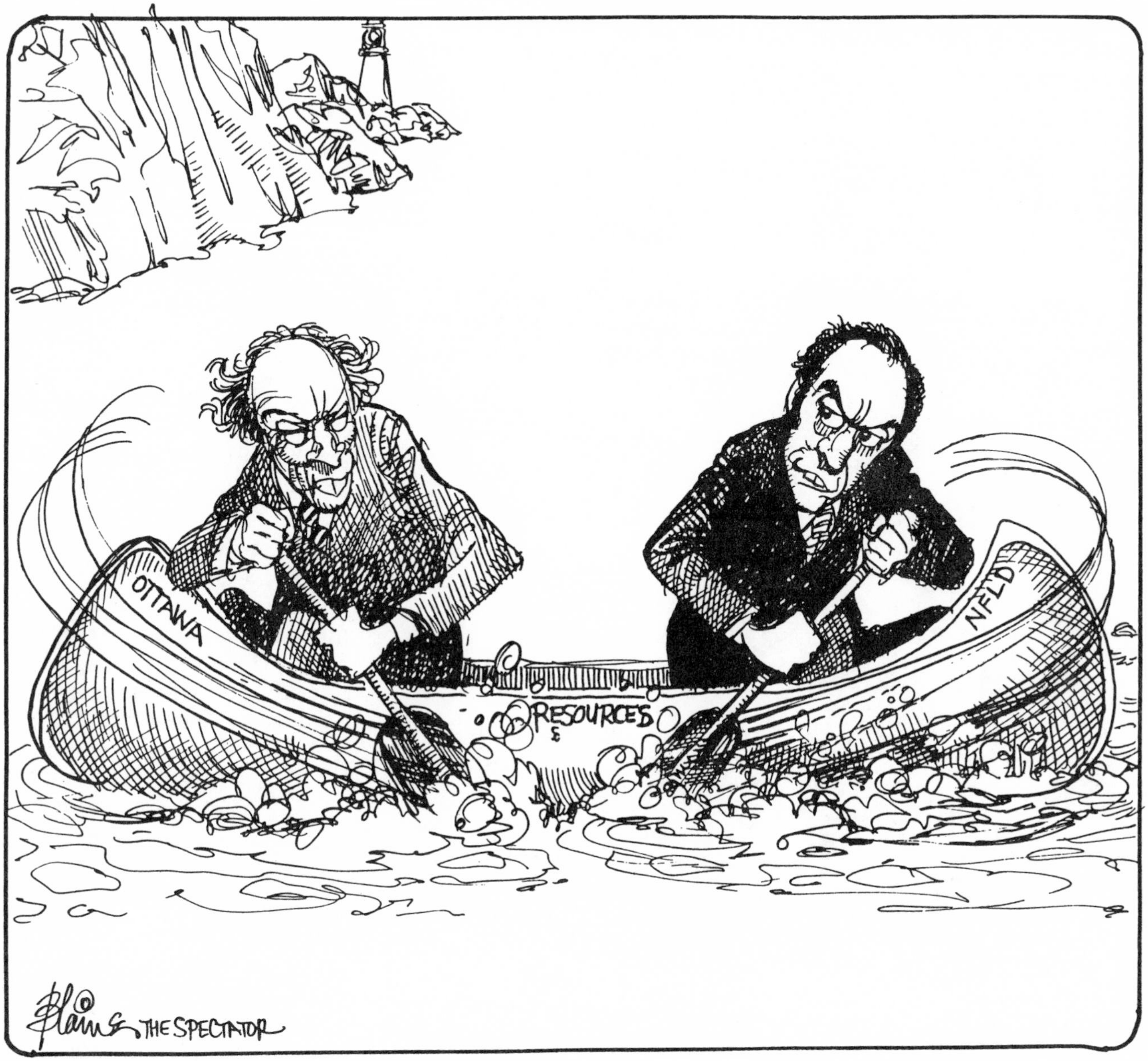
OTTAWA
NFLD
RESOURCES
THE SPECTATOR

"Every man has his own reasons, I suppose, as driving forces, but mine were twofold: one, to make sure that Quebec wouldn't leave Canada through separation, and the other was to make sure that Canada wouldn't shove Quebec out through narrowmindedness."
—Pierre Elliott Trudeau
CTV "W5" Interview, *December 21, 1973*
from Trudeau *by George Radwanski*

"Bilingualism is not an imposition on the citizens. The citizens can go on speaking one language or six languages or no languages if they so choose. Bilingualism is an imposition on the state and not on the citizens."
—Pierre Elliott Trudeau, 1966
from Trudeau *by George Radwanski*

REIDFORD
THE GLOBE AND MAIL, OCTOBER 21, 1969

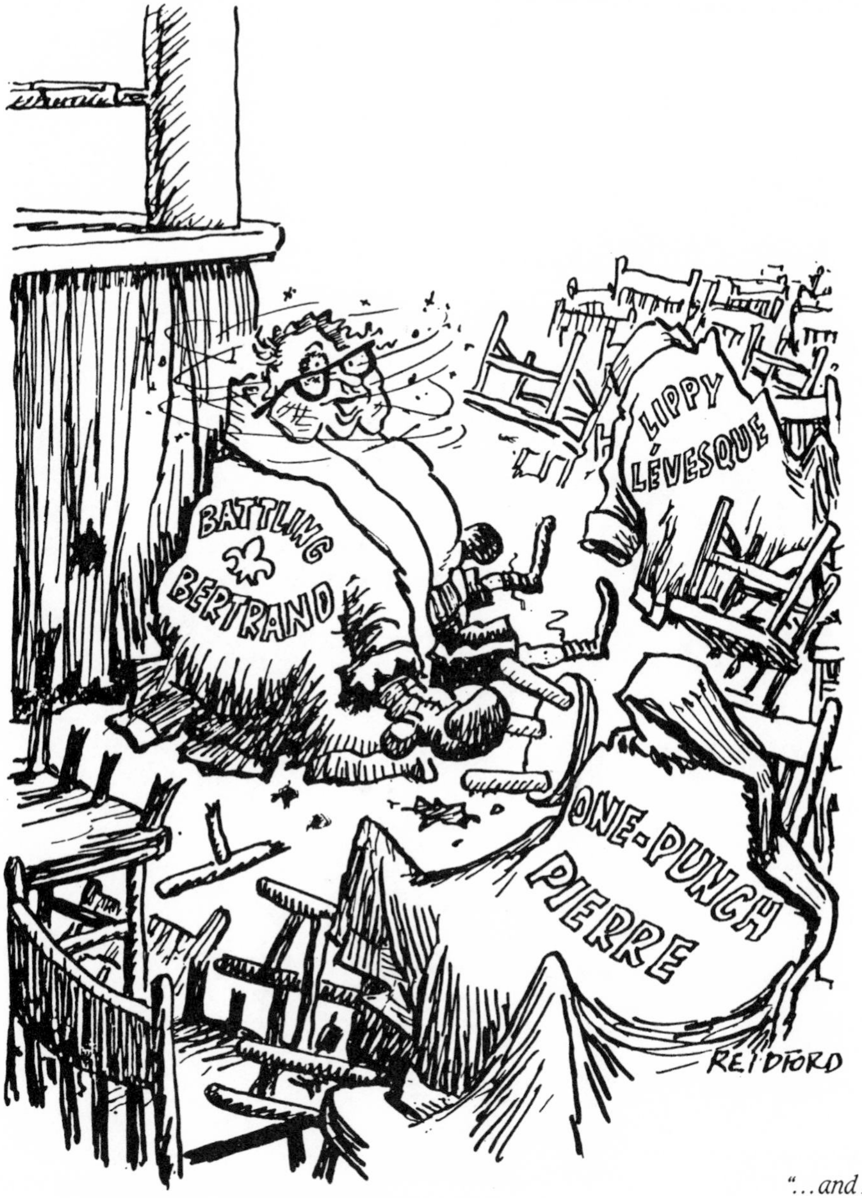
BATTLING BERTRAND
LIPPY LÉVESQUE
ONE-PUNCH PIERRE
REIDFORD

"... and I haven't even entered the ring!"

"He always knows where he stands on an issue. If you don't have that sense of certainty in politics, the pressures and compromises soon destroy you."
—*"a Quebec colleague of Trudeau"*
quoted by Peter Desbarats
in Saturday Night, *June 1975*

FRANKLIN
THE GLOBE AND MAIL, FEBRUARY 22, 1975

Quebec Connection

"Politics is a great game and you try to outfox
people. Resourcefulness is something I have
pleasure in observing and using."
—*Pierre Elliott Trudeau, September 28, 1978*
from Grits *by Christina McCall Newman*

"If in order to solve a little problem of
language, and I put it deliberately in those
terms, we have to bust up the country, we don't
have much genius in this country."
—*Pierre Elliott Trudeau in an interview*
with Jack Webster, July 6, 1977

ANDY DONATO
THE TORONTO SUN

ANY SUGGESTIONS FOR THE NEW CONSTITUTION?
NON!
DONATO
TORONTO SUN

"No state is eternal. The only thing that will keep us together is the will to stay together."
—Pierre Elliott Trudeau
February, 1979

"Levesque's election victory elevated Trudeau's status to that of Saviour of Canada: within a year his Gallup Poll standing went from 29 per cent to 51 per cent."
—Richard Gwyn
Northern Magus

"...the judgement of time will applaud Trudeau for what is currently regarded as his greatest failure: Quebec... his brave and stubborn determination to impose official bilingualism on an ostensibly bilingual country (with a streak of prejudice still running underground) probably stalled the progress of the *independantistes*."
—Allan Fotheringham
Malice in Blunderland

ADRIAN RAESIDE
TIMES-COLONIST, NOVEMBER 16, 1981

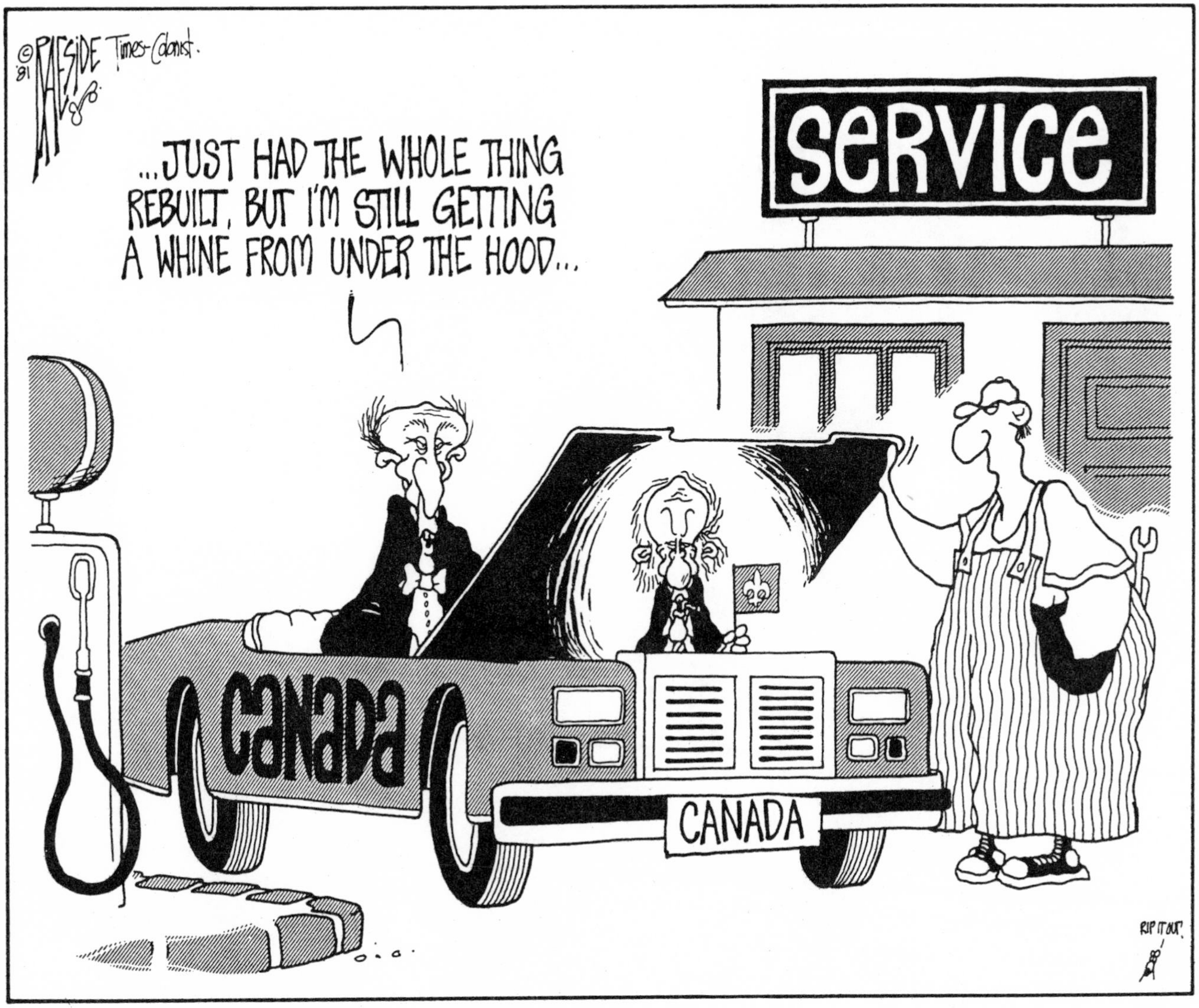
©'81 RAESIDE Times-Colonist
...JUST HAD THE WHOLE THING REBUILT, BUT I'M STILL GETTING A WHINE FROM UNDER THE HOOD...
SERVICE
CANADA
CANADA
RIP IT OUT!

"A natural born talent for getting slapped in the face."

—Rene Levesque on Trudeau
from Rene: A Canadian in Search of a Country
by Peter Desbarats

MIKE GRASTON
THE WINDSOR STAR, JUNE 18, 1982

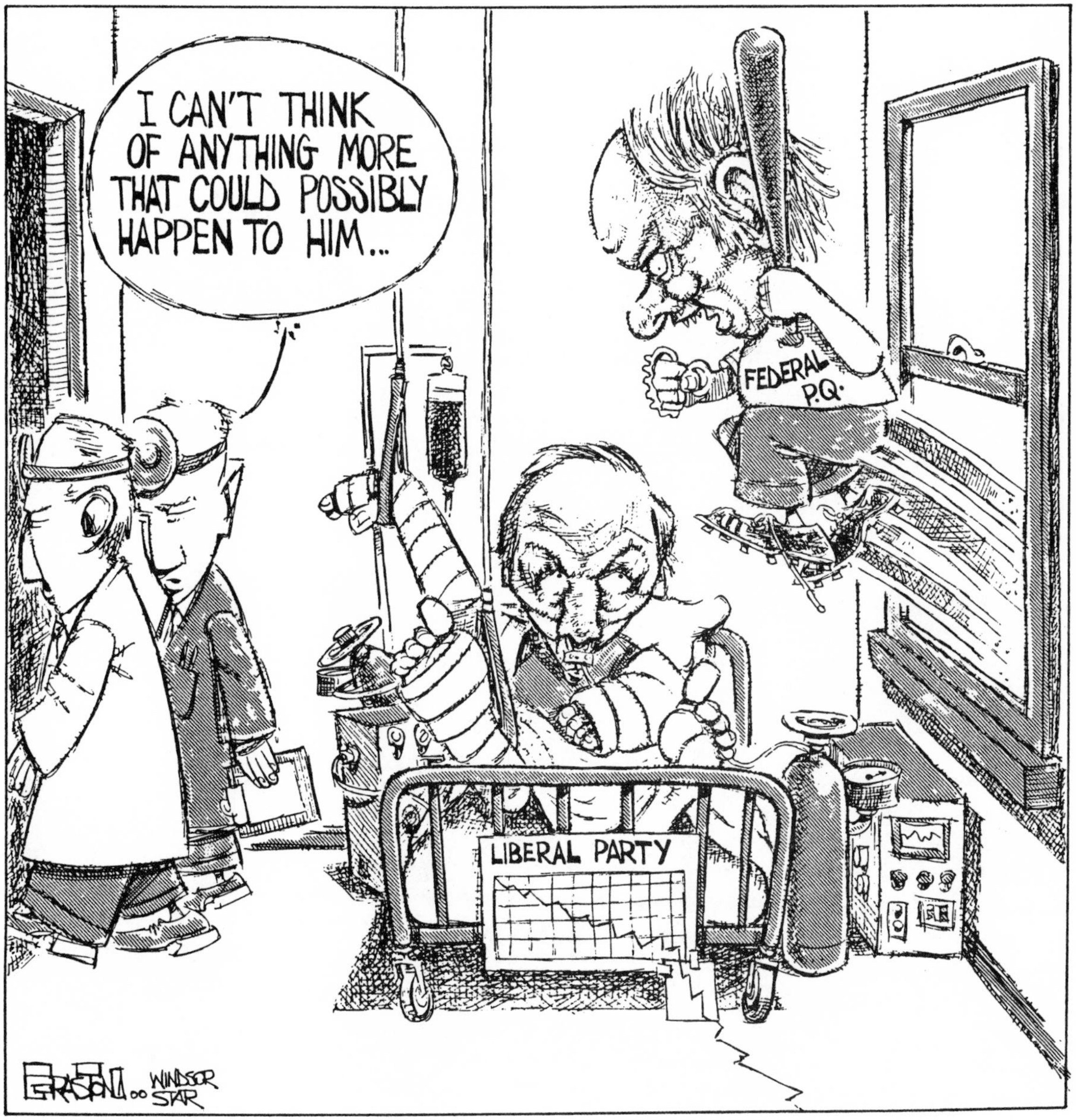
I CAN'T THINK OF ANYTHING MORE THAT COULD POSSIBLY HAPPEN TO HIM...
FEDERAL P.Q.
LIBERAL PARTY
WINDSOR STAR

"On many levels, the Trudeau-Levesque confrontation has about it a mythic aura."
—*Christina McCall Newman*
in Saturday Night, *January February, 1977*

AISLIN
MONTREAL GAZETTE, MAY 22, 1980

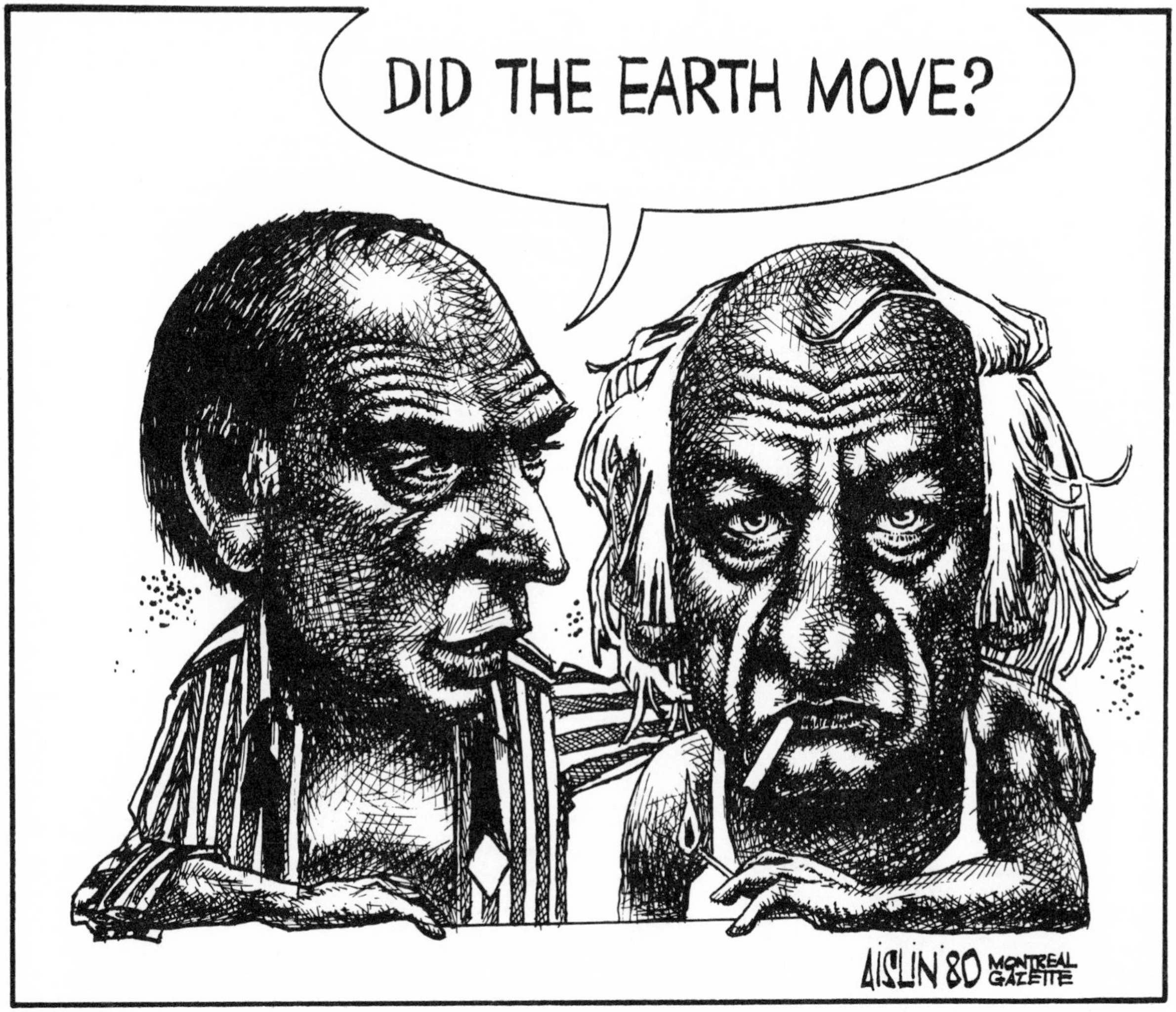
DID THE EARTH MOVE?
AISLIN '80 MONTREAL GAZETTE

"You can't weigh Trudeau on ordinary scales.
It isn't just that he's brilliant— Arthur Meighen
was easily his equal in brains— but that there
clings to him something mysterious, which for
want of a better word I'll call 'luck.' Fortune has
a way of turning in his favour. For him the
centre holds."
—Conservative Senator Grattan O'Leary
quoted by Christina McCall Newman
in Saturday Night, *January February, 1977*

EDD ULUSCHAK
EDMONTON JOURNAL, AUGUST 29, 1980

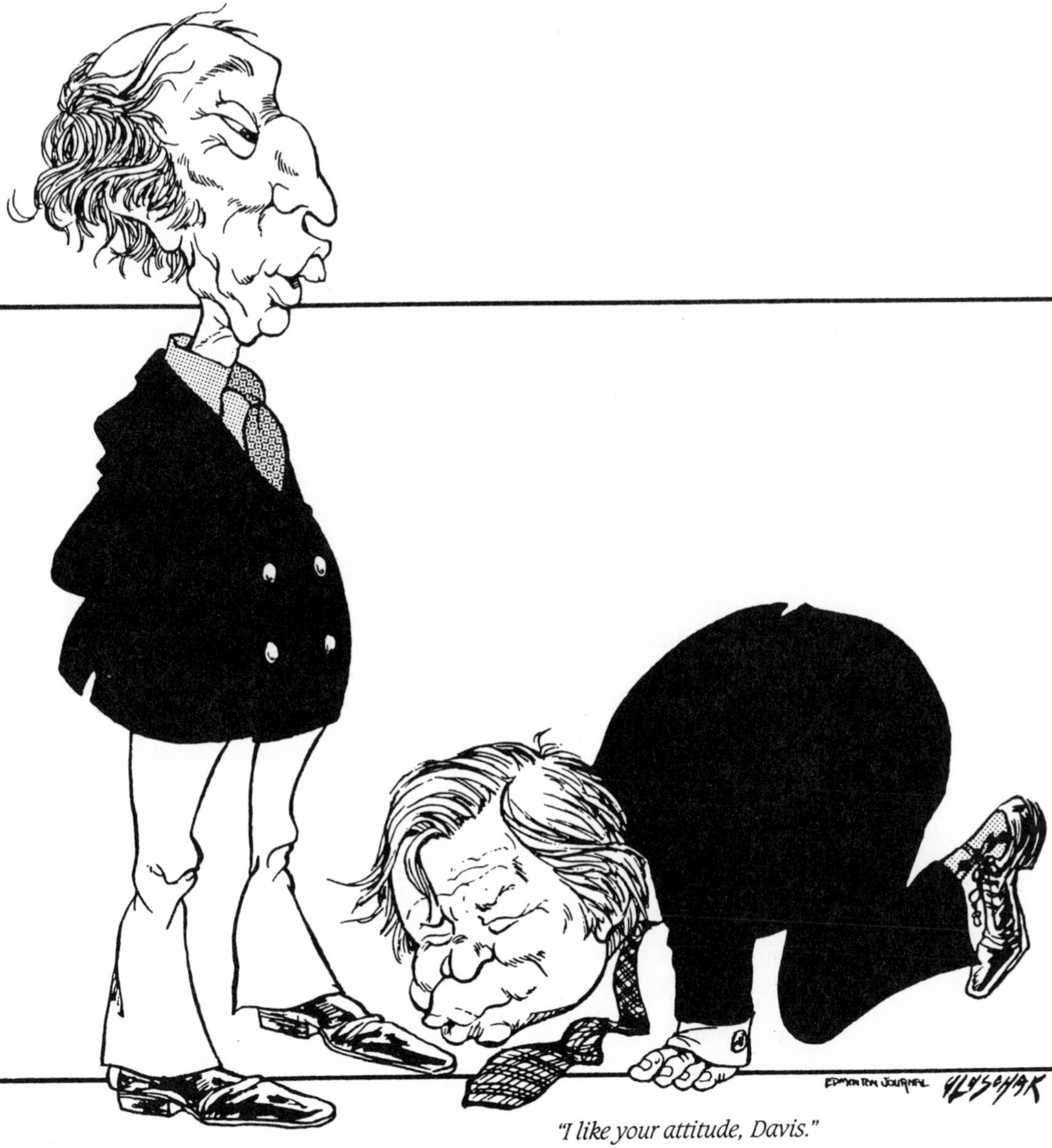
EDMONTON JOURNAL
ULUSCHAK

"I like your attitude, Davis."

"The theory of checks and balance has always had my full support. It translates into practical terms the concept of equilibrium that is inseparable from freedom in the realm of ideas. It incorporates a corrective for abuses and excesses into the very functioning of political institutions. My political action, or my theory — insomuch as I can be said to have one — can be expressed very simply: create counterweights."

—Pierre Elliott Trudeau
Federalism and the French Canadians

EDD ULUSCHAK
EDMONTON JOURNAL, MARCH 21, 1980

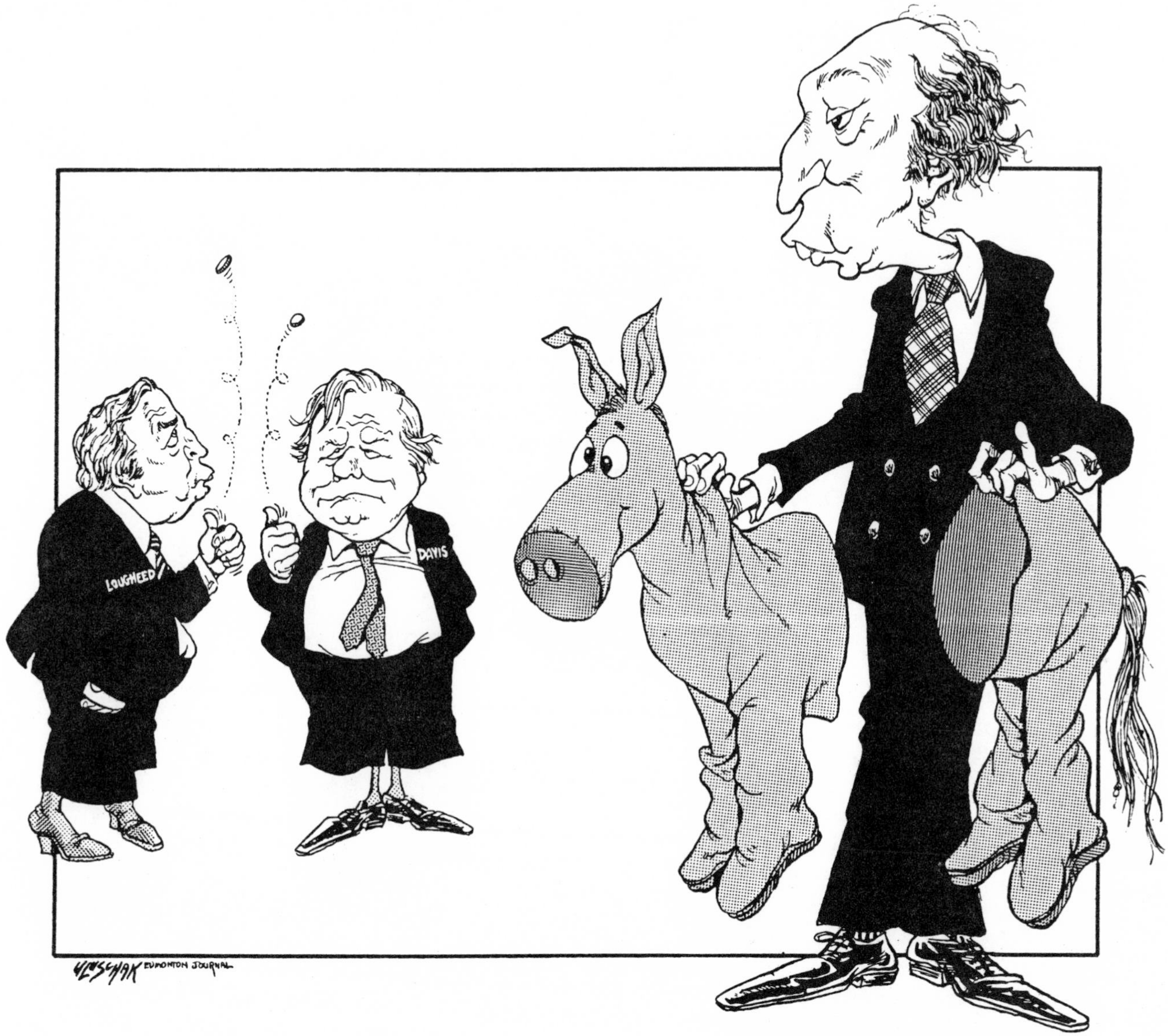
LOUGHEED
DAVIS
EDMONTON JOURNAL

"It's a cliche that hate is the flip side of love, or of love rejected. Beyond any doubt, Trudeau obsessed Westerners, and in this sense he dominated them as well. In election after election they did not so much cast their ballots as hurl them against him."

—*Richard Gwyn,* The Toronto Star
March 1, 1984

FRANKLIN
THE GLOBE AND MAIL, MARCH 6, 1974

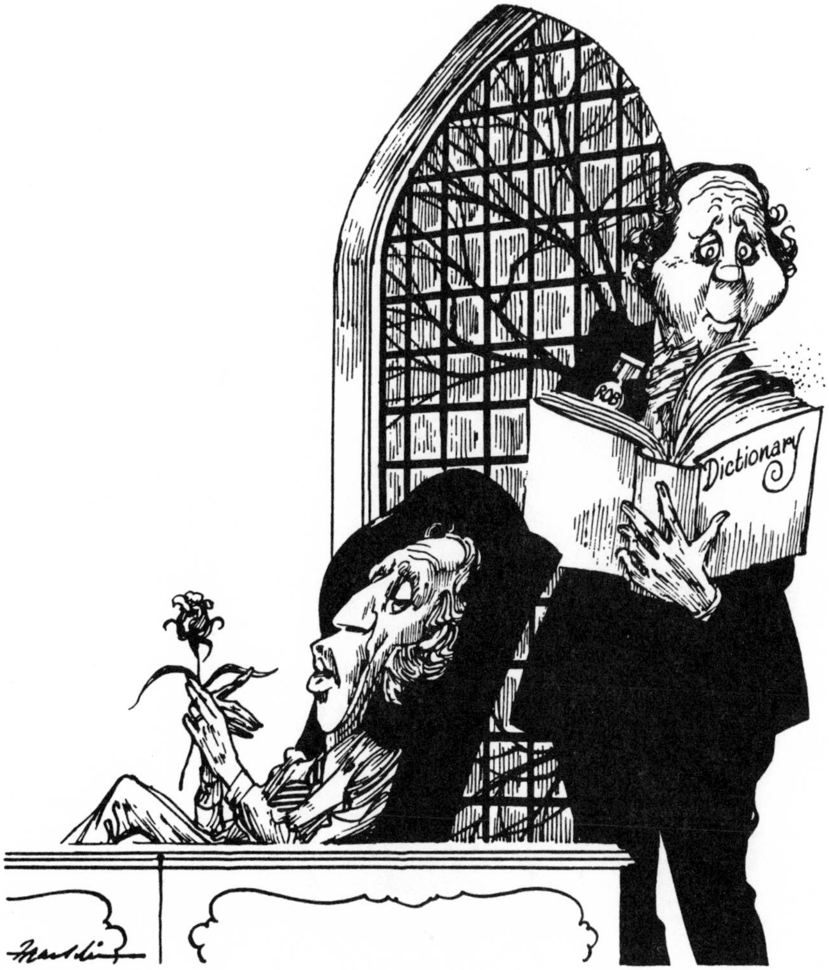
Dictionary

"Quid pro quo *is Latin for Lougheed socks it to us and we sock it to him."*

"It's not a perfect job, but it sure beats working."

—Pierre Elliott Trudeau
on being prime minister
October 8, 1975

ANDY DONATO
THE TORONTO SUN

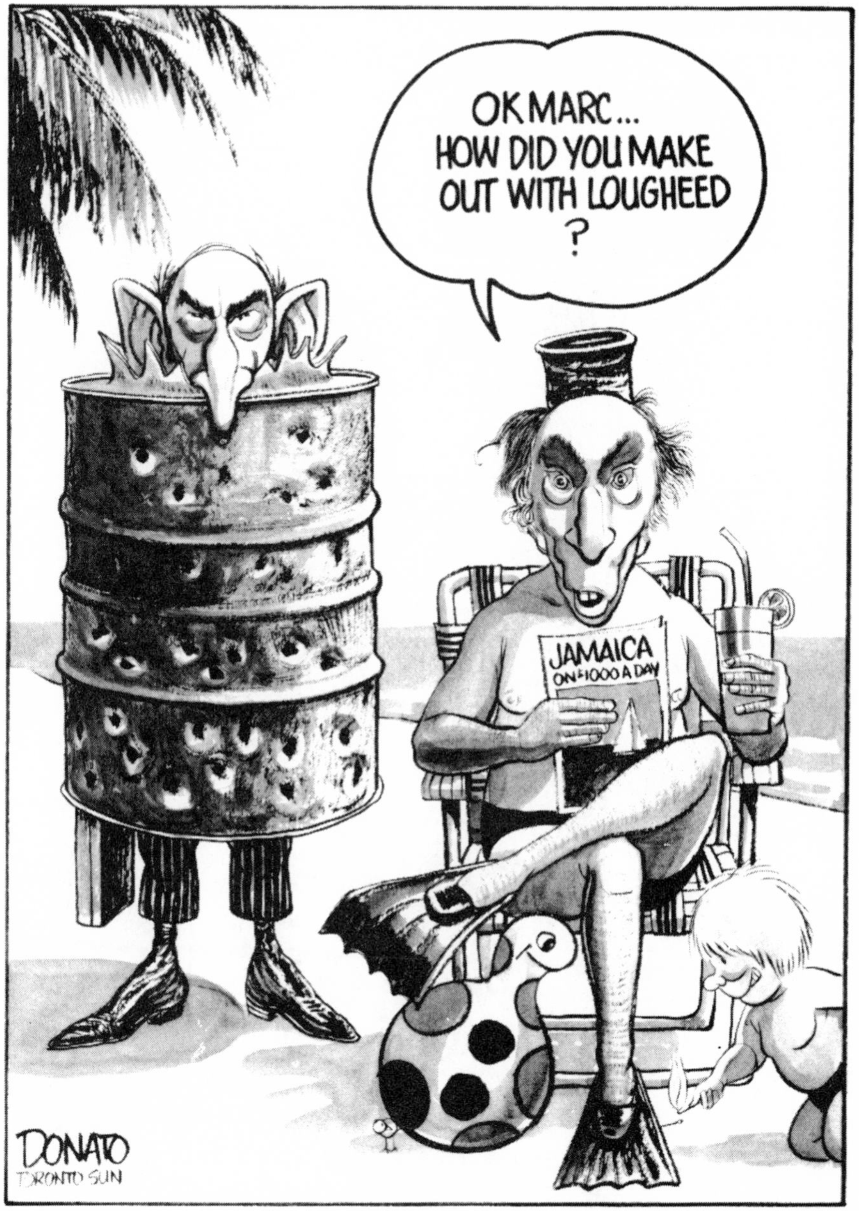
OK MARC...
HOW DID YOU MAKE
OUT WITH LOUGHEED
?
JAMAICA
ON $1000 A DAY
DONATO
TORONTO SUN

I'LL COME UP A LITTLE AND PEG THE PRICE OF OIL ABOUT HERE...OK?
NO WAY...I THINK IT SHOULD BE ABOUT HERE!
THAT'S A LITTLE TOO HIGH... HOW'BOUT WE SETTLE FOR AROUND HERE?
TOO LOW PAL...LET'S TRY IT ABOUT HERE!
DONATO TORONTO SUN

ANDY DONATO
THE TORONTO SUN, JULY 24, 1980

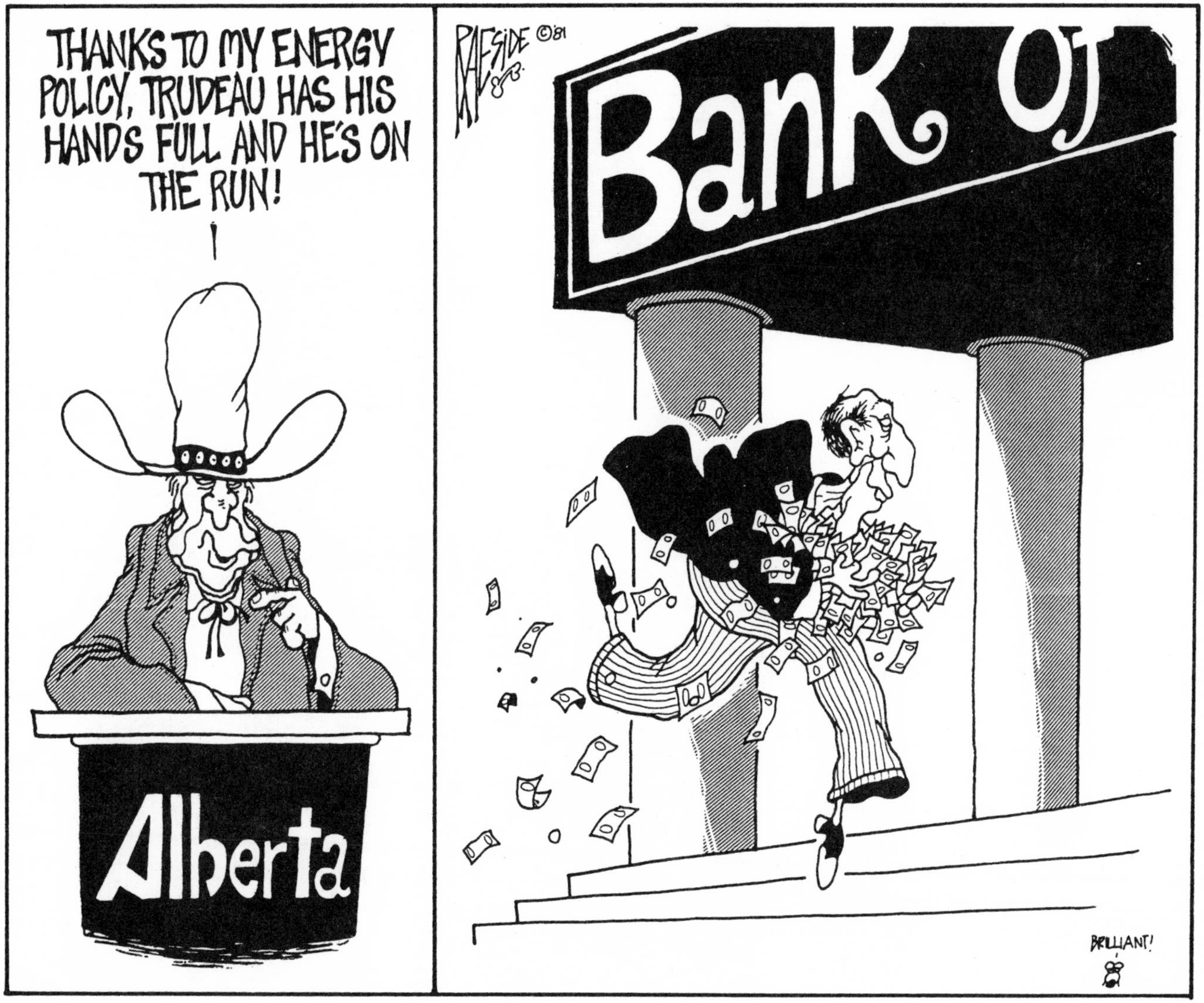
THANKS TO MY ENERGY POLICY, TRUDEAU HAS HIS HANDS FULL AND HE'S ON THE RUN!
RAESIDE ©81
Bank of
Alberta
BRILLIANT!

ADRIAN RAESIDE
TIMES-COLONIST

An interesting out-of-context quote that continues to be used against Trudeau— "Well, why should I sell the Canadian farmers' wheat?" (Winnipeg, December 13, 1968)— was actually uttered in a speech essentially saying that he didn't need to help because he felt that farmers were getting along very well without further government intervention.

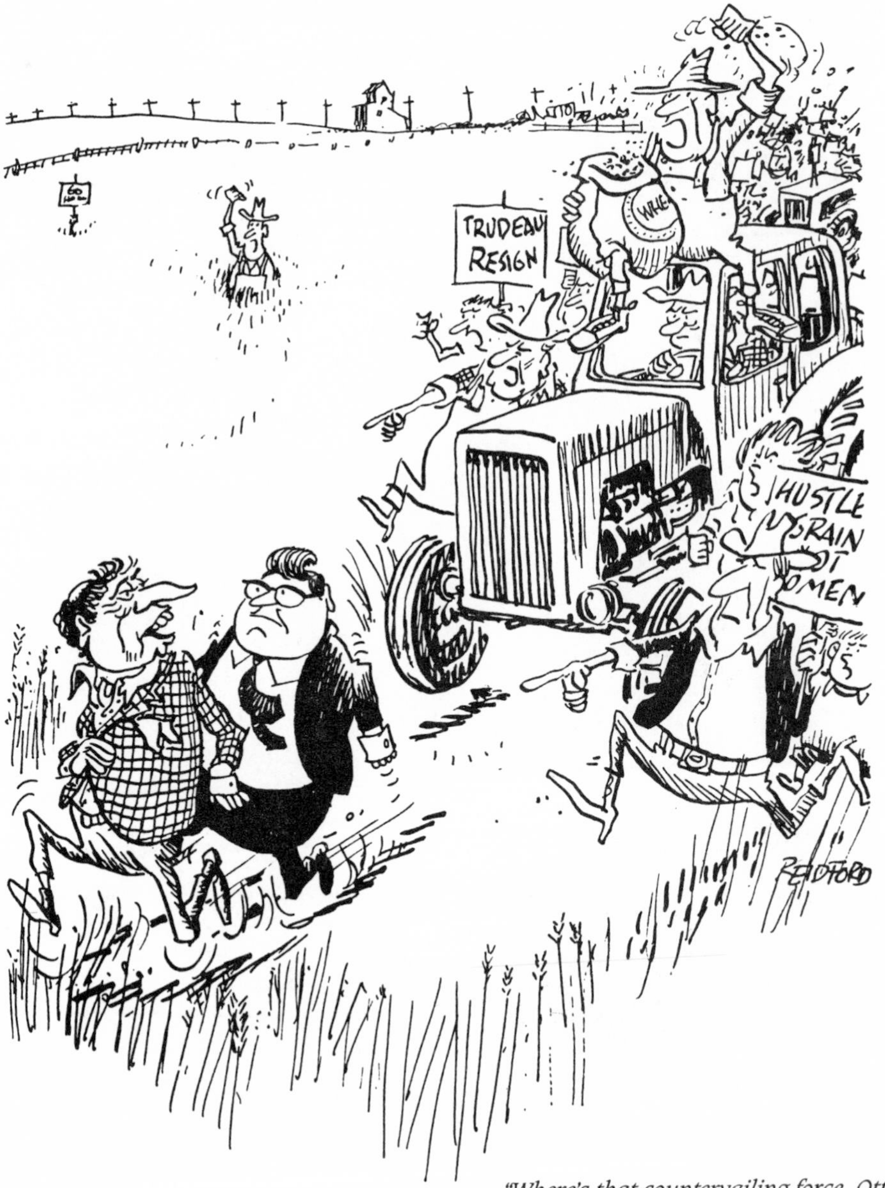
TRUDEAU RESIGN
REIDFORD

REIDFORD
THE GLOBE AND MAIL, JULY 18, 1969

"Where's that countervailing force, Otto?"

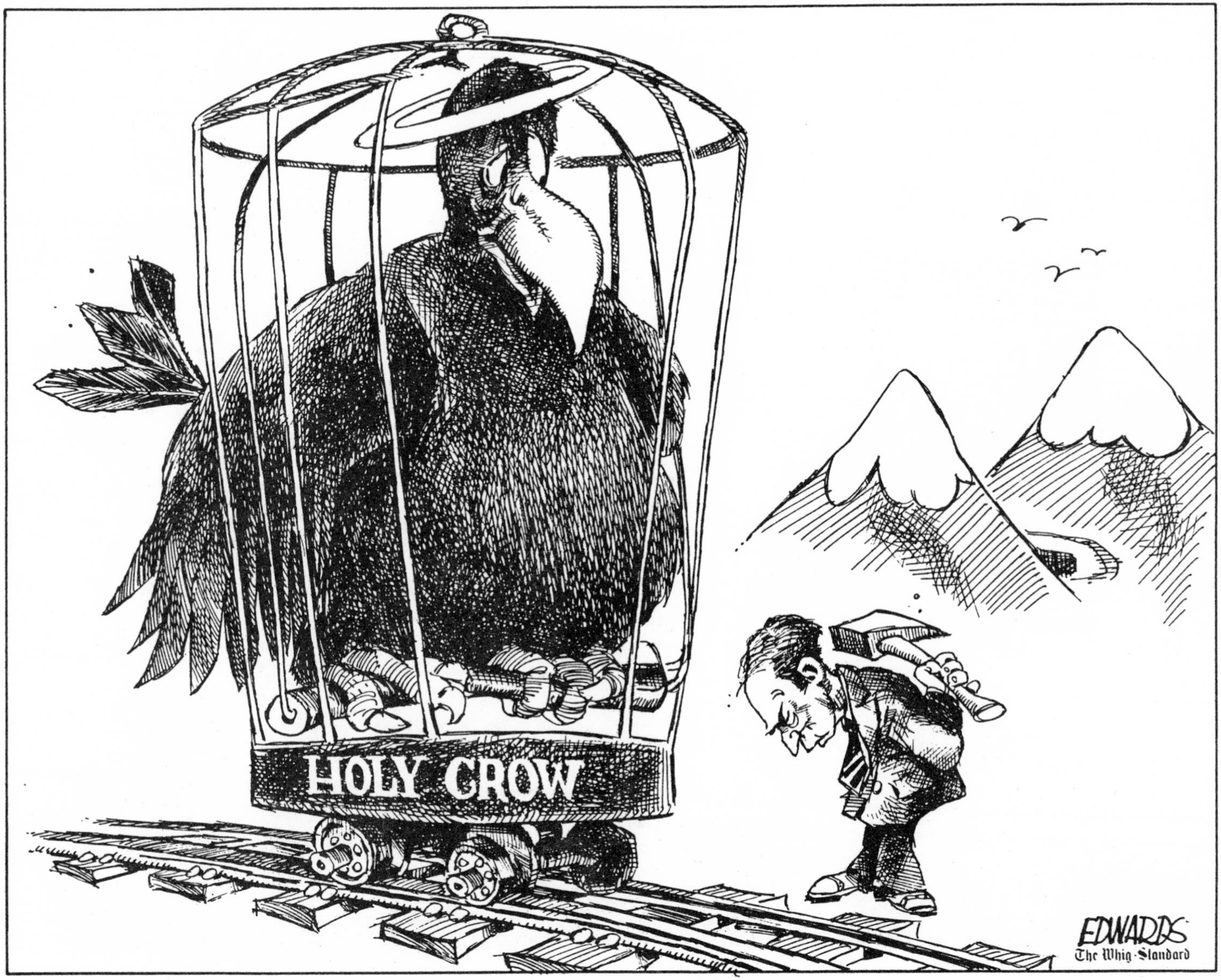
HOLY CROW
EDWARDS
The Whig-Standard

FRANK EDWARDS
THE WHIG-STANDARD, MAY 25, 1983

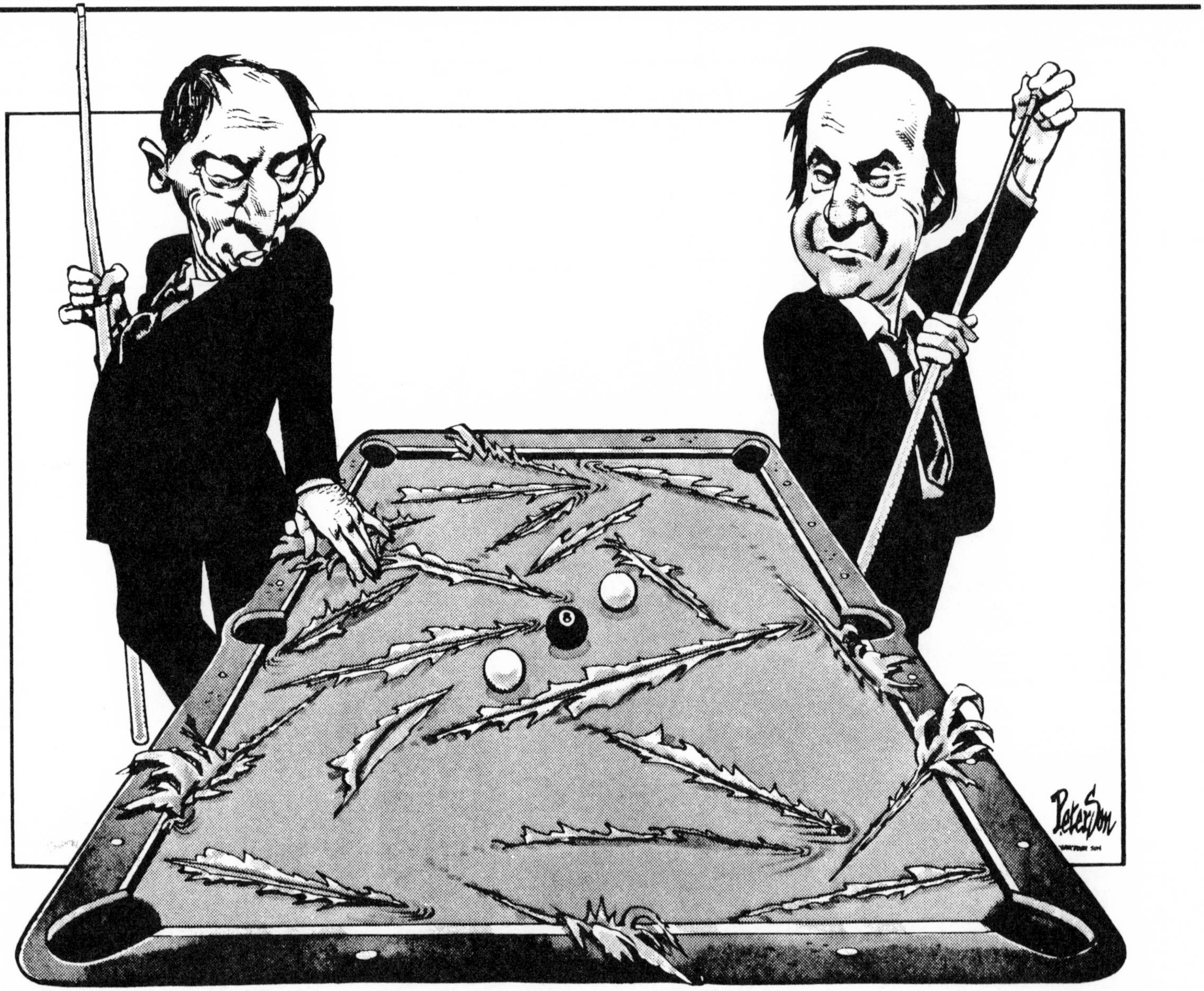
Peterson

ROY PETERSON
VANCOUVER SUN, OCTOBER 15, 1981

"I put a position on the table and Premier Bennett is going to talk to his fellow premiers and he [Bennett] put a position on the table and I'll think about it." —Pierre Trudeau, Oct. 14, 1981

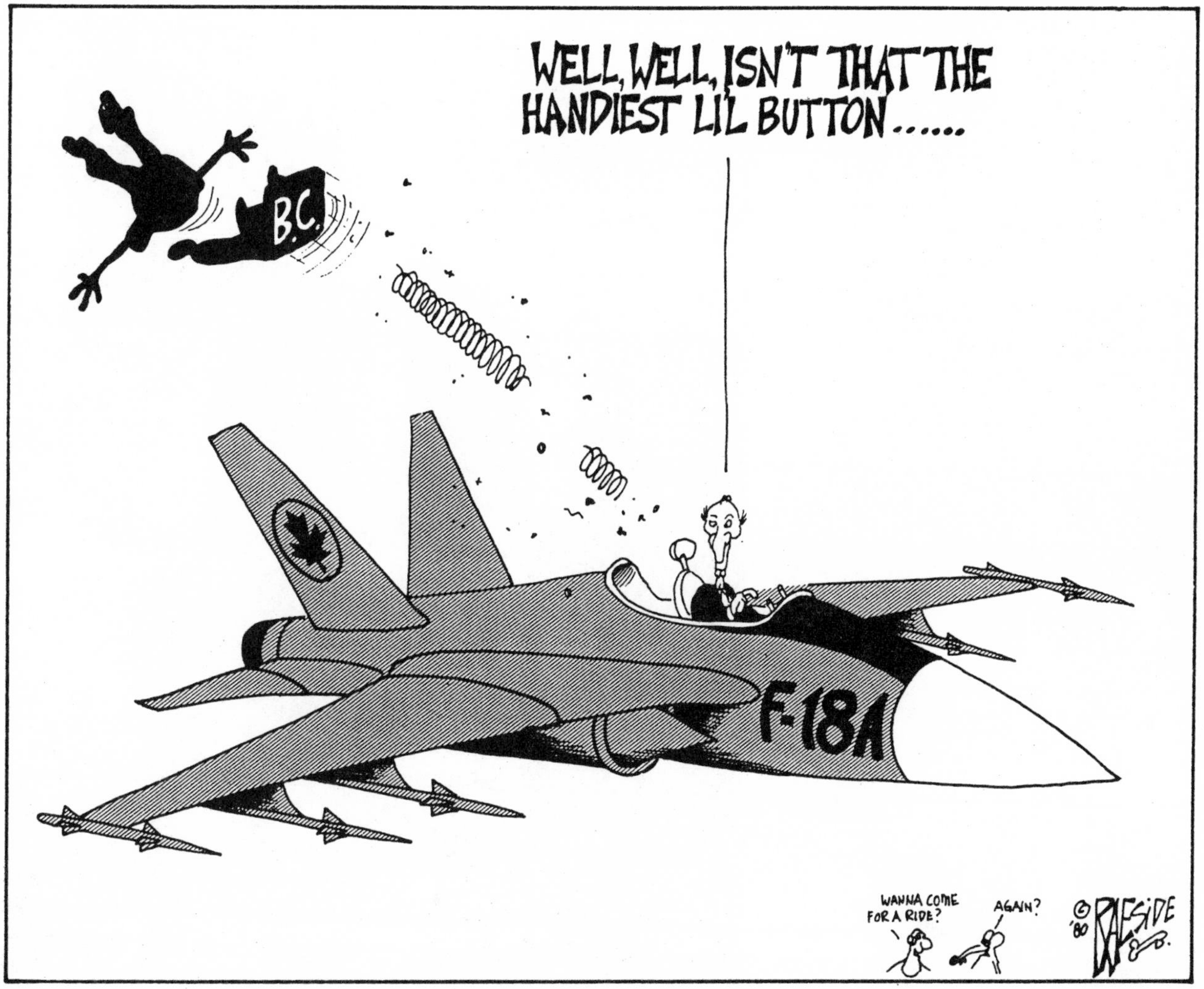
WELL, WELL, ISN'T THAT THE HANDIEST LI'L BUTTON......
B.C.
F-18A
WANNA COME FOR A RIDE?
AGAIN?
© '80 RAESIDE

ADRIAN RAESIDE
TIMES-COLONIST, APRIL 18, 1980

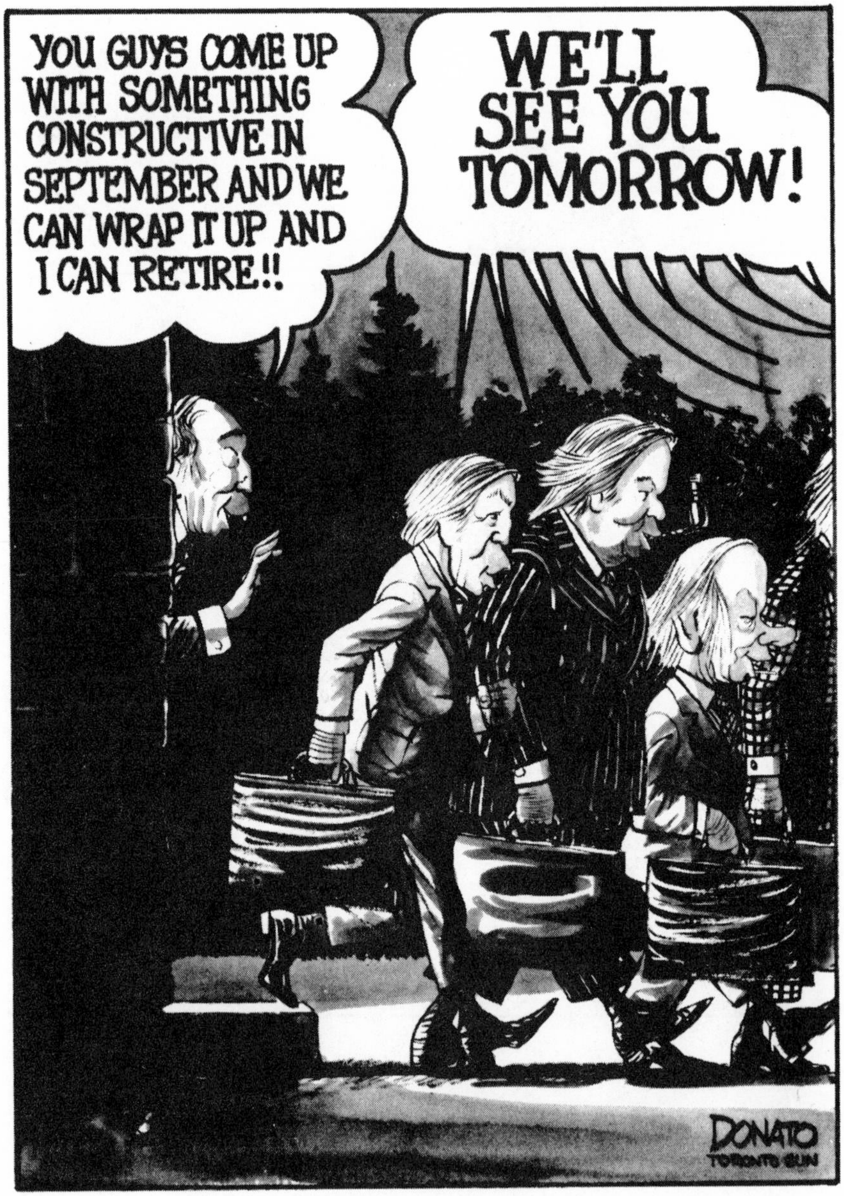
YOU GUYS COME UP WITH SOMETHING CONSTRUCTIVE IN SEPTEMBER AND WE CAN WRAP IT UP AND I CAN RETIRE!!
WE'LL SEE YOU TOMORROW!
DONATO TORONTO SUN

ANDY DONATO
THE TORONTO SUN

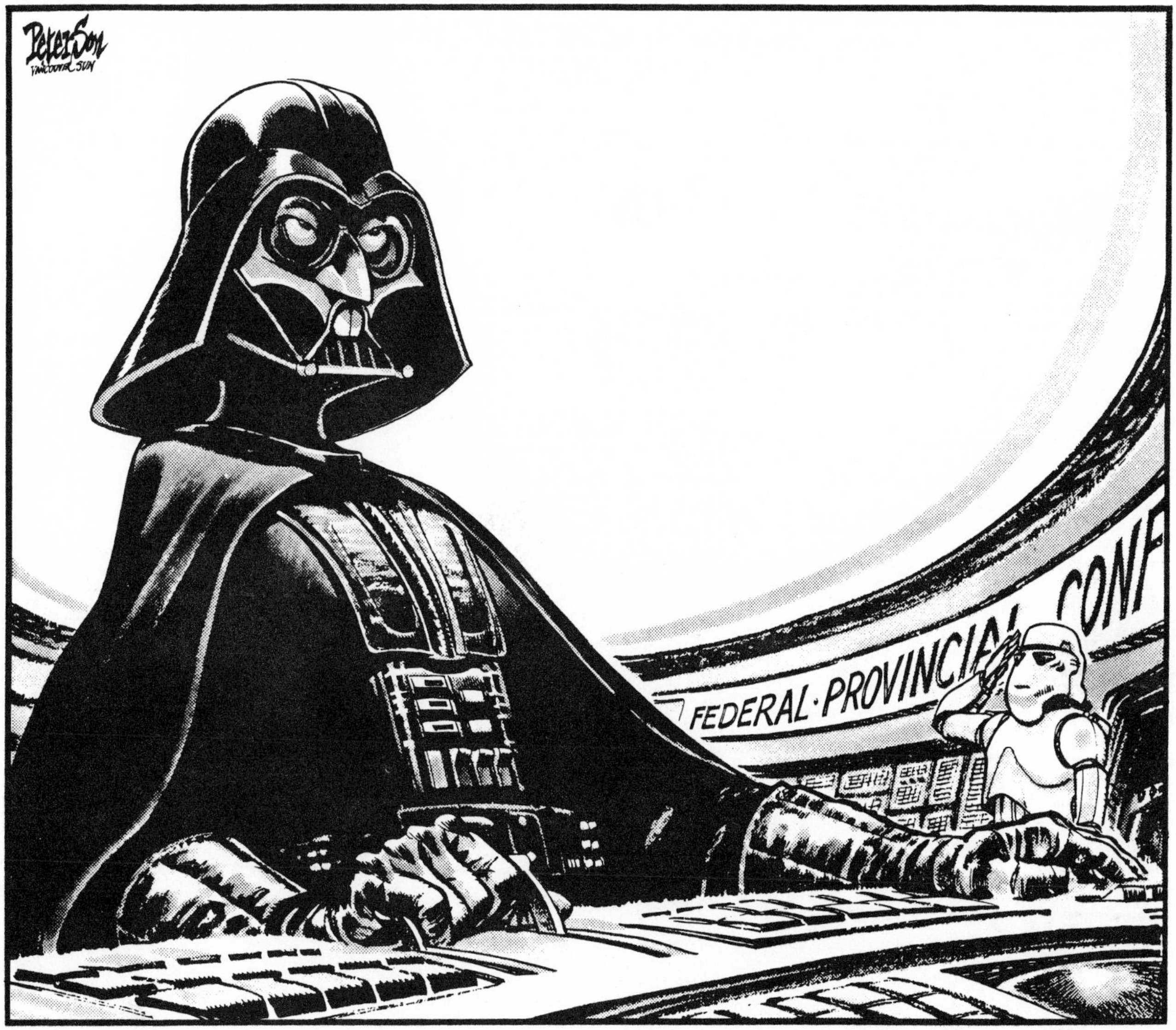
PETERSON
VANCOUVER SUN
FEDERAL·PROVINCIAL CONF

ROY PETERSON
VANCOUVER SUN, AUGUST 5, 1983

"We must put an end to this inter-empire fed-bashing. Have my love letters to the premiers been received? Good...now stand by to nuke 'em with the cruise just in case..."

POLITICS

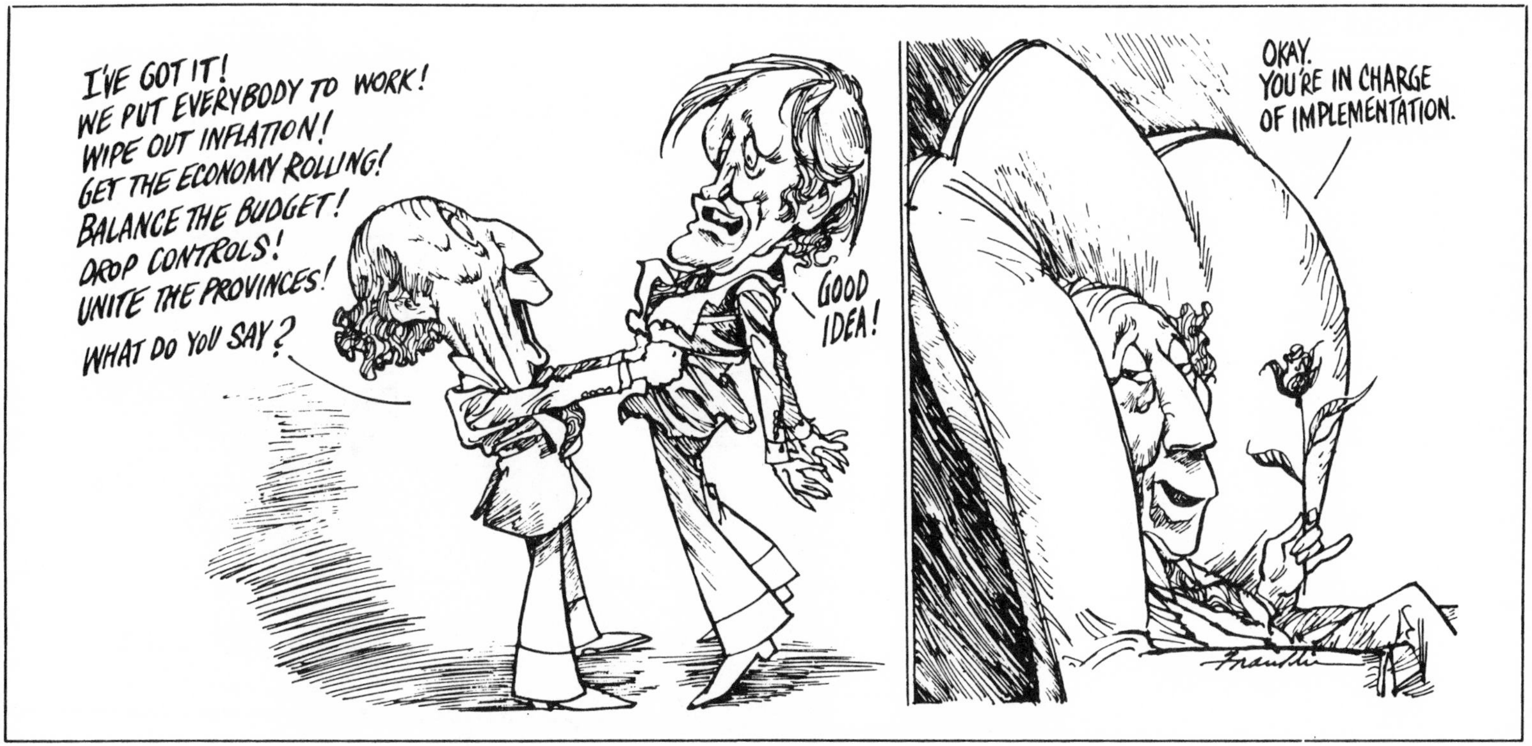
I'VE GOT IT!
WE PUT EVERYBODY TO WORK!
WIPE OUT INFLATION!
GET THE ECONOMY ROLLING!
BALANCE THE BUDGET!
DROP CONTROLS!
UNITE THE PROVINCES!
WHAT DO YOU SAY?
GOOD IDEA!
OKAY.
YOU'RE IN CHARGE
OF IMPLEMENTATION.
Franklin

FRANKLIN
THE GLOBE AND MAIL, OCTOBER 15, 1977

"Prior to the economic crisis of the mid-1970s, Pierre Trudeau had maintained the traditional optimism concerning the performance of the Canadian economy. His economic addresses were classical statements of the Canadian liberal conception of society and economic strategy. Like former Liberal leaders he depended for political success on combining policies to promote an expanding free-enterprise economy with visions of improved social services and higher wages and salaries for ordinary Canadians."

—James Laxer and Robert Laxer
from The Liberal Idea of Canada

"Inflation has been beaten."
—Pierre Elliott Trudeau
August, 1972

FRANKLIN
THE GLOBE AND MAIL, JANUARY 2, 1971

"Hmmm, and for the economy I predict..."

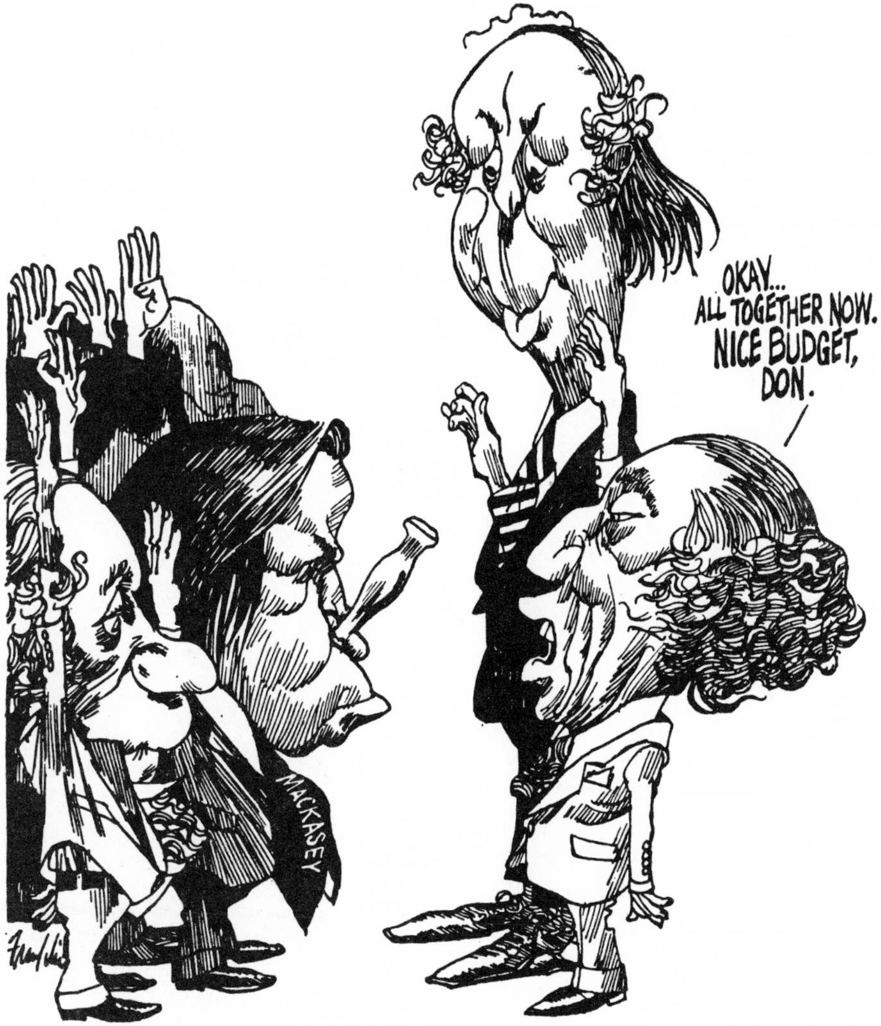
OKAY...
ALL TOGETHER NOW.
NICE BUDGET,
DON.
MACKASEY

FRANKLIN
THE GLOBE AND MAIL, MAY 29, 1976

"I'm not worried about your criticisms, I'm really not.

"A budget is a passing thing. There will be another budget next year that you can complain about."

—Pierre Elliott Trudeau
November 21, 1981

ADRIAN RAESIDE
TIMES-COLONIST, OCTOBER 15, 1980

I'M GONNA PUT A HIDEOUS CURSE ON YOU THAT WILL LEAVE YOU ETERNALLY DAMNED!
ZAPPO!
BUDGET
©'80 RAESIDE

"He's a rather conservative economist. On the
financial side, he's a Scot, a conservative, a
penny saved is a penny earned."

—Marc Lalonde
from Trudeau *by George Radwanski*

EDD ULUSCHAK
EDMONTON JOURNAL, FEBRUARY 17, 1982

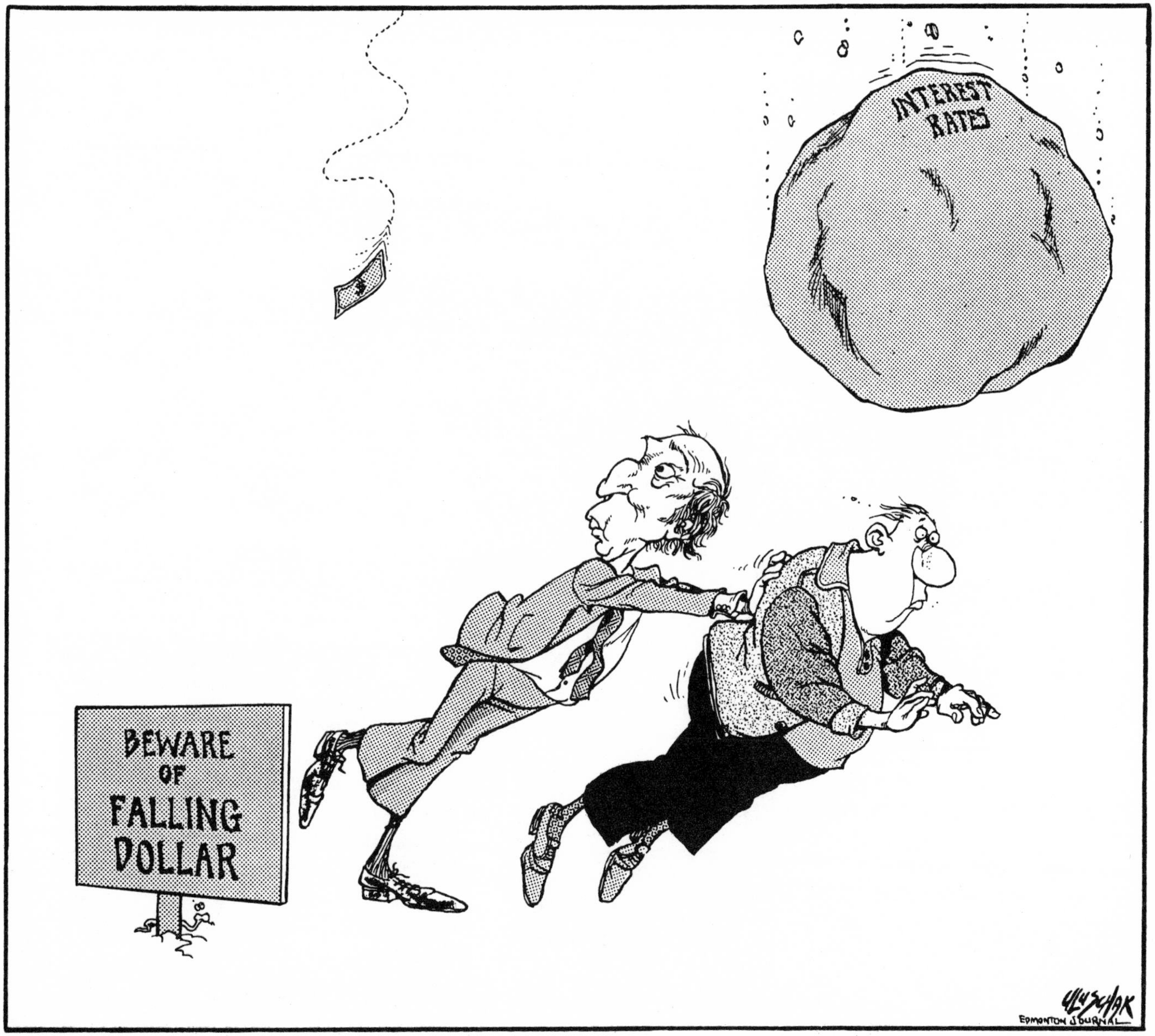
INTEREST RATES
BEWARE OF FALLING DOLLAR
ULUSCHAK
EDMONTON JOURNAL

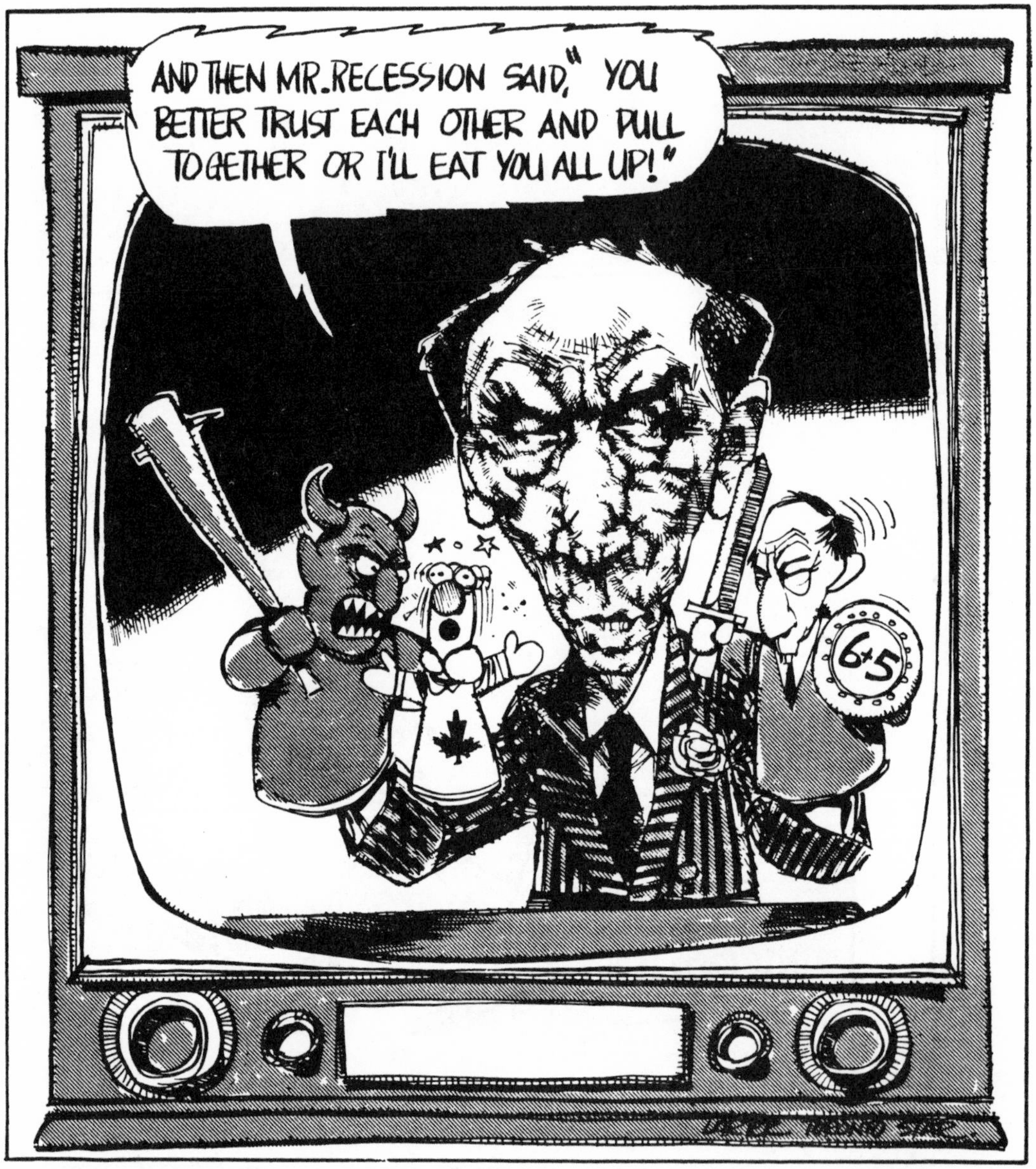
AND THEN MR. RECESSION SAID, " YOU BETTER TRUST EACH OTHER AND PULL TOGETHER OR I'LL EAT YOU ALL UP!"
6+5

JOHN LARTER
THE TORONTO STAR, OCTOBER 22, 1982

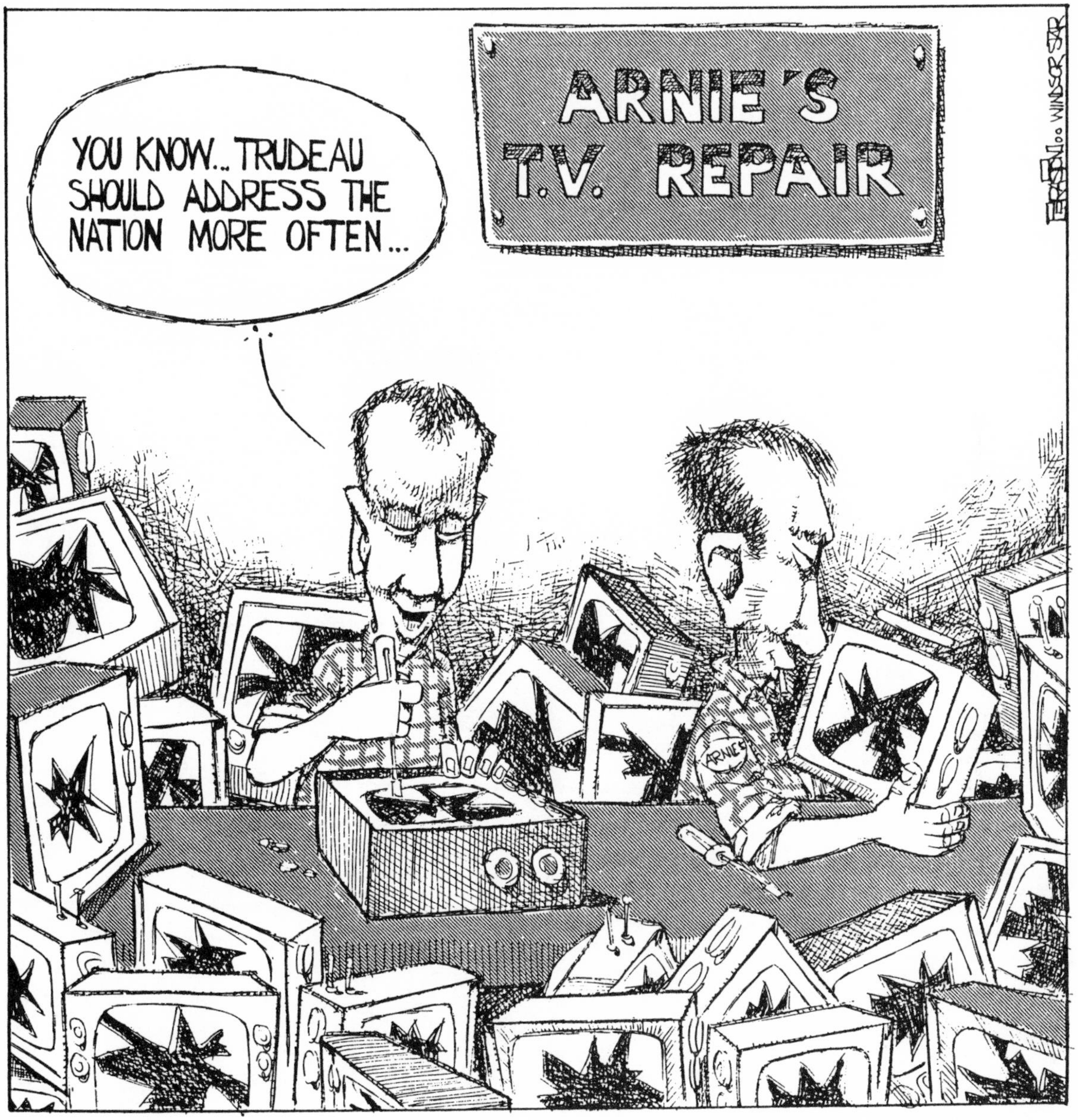
ARNIE'S
T.V. REPAIR
YOU KNOW... TRUDEAU SHOULD ADDRESS THE NATION MORE OFTEN...
ARNIE'S

MIKE GRASTON
VANCOUVER SUN, OCTOBER 25, 1982

"More important than the economic controls established by the government was the accompanying attempt by the Prime Minister to initiate a new public morality for Canada. This morality was not the product of Pierre Trudeau's fevered thinking in the face of Canada's economic troubles. It was nothing less than a new liberalism for Canada... an ideology of restraint."

—James Laxer and Robert Laxer
from The Liberal Idea of Canada

FRANK EDWARDS
THE WHIG-STANDARD

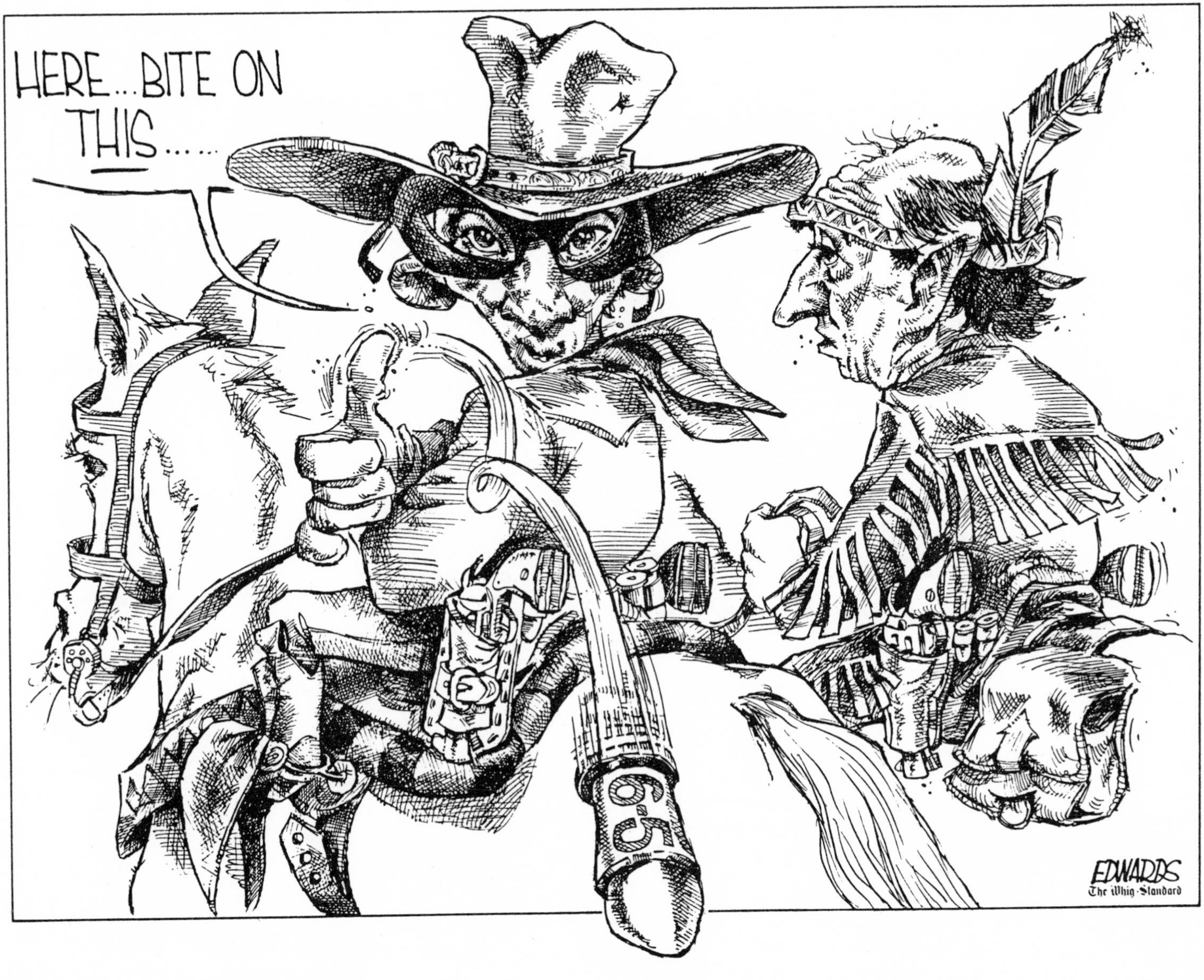
HERE...BITE ON THIS......
'65
EDWARDS
The Whig-Standard

"No one liked discussion more than Pierre Trudeau. He is a born seminar leader... No one was more tolerant of the right of discussion than Trudeau, but nobody was less sympathetic to ideas he thought irrelevant, unsound or unintelligible."

—Paul Martin
from A Very Public Life

"...he tolerated the comings and goings of misguided ministers from his cabinet with all the gusto of a Coney Island ticket taker."
—Robert Lewis, Maclean's

FRANKLIN
THE GLOBE AND MAIL, OCTOBER 15, 1976

GET ME MITCH, PLEASE.

MR. SHARP RESIGNED RECENTLY.

I WANT TO SEE DRURY IMMEDIATELY.

SORRY, SIR, MR. DRURY HAS RESIGNED.

TELL MACKASEY I WANT TO SEE HIM...

HE QUIT, REMEMBER?

John
Jim

CALL THIS NUMBER.

BUT THIS IS YOUR NUMBER.

I KNOW... JUST CHECKING.

"If there is anything that puzzles me in this game, it is that the longer that you are in the job of Prime Minister, the harder you have to work to do your job. With anything else, such as stenography, administering a store, or whatever... you get to know the ropes pretty well and it becomes easy and you can spend a lot of time playing golf or something. I feel that the more you know, the more you have to know and the more problems come at you. It is certainly not because I do not delegate."
—*Pierre Elliott Trudeau,*
October 6, 1977 in a Montreal Star
interview from Pierre Elliott Trudeau
by Charles Bordeleau

AISLIN
MONTREAL GAZETTE, DECEMBER 5, 1978

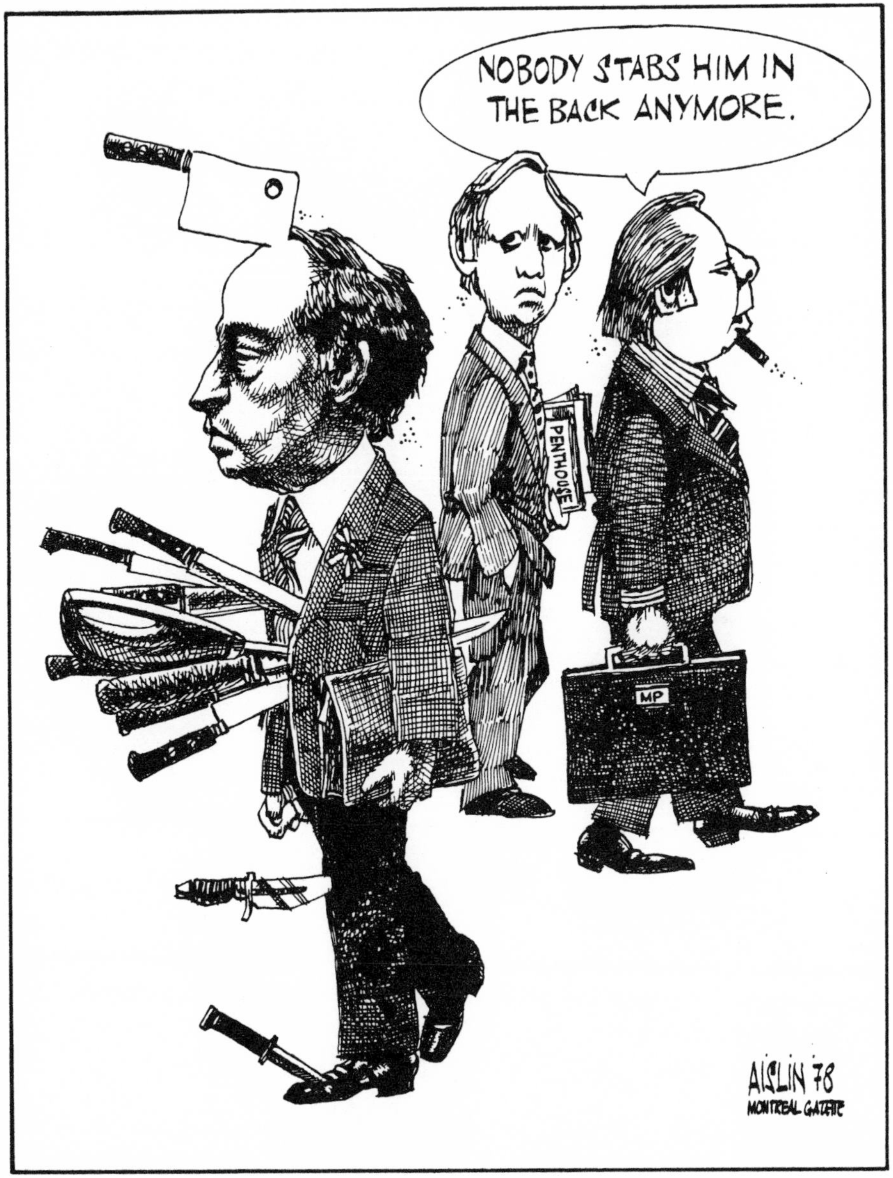
NOBODY STABS HIM IN THE BACK ANYMORE.
PENTHOUSE
MP
AISLIN 78
MONTREAL GAZETTE

"My father taught me order and discipline,
and my mother, freedom and fantasy."
—Pierre Elliott Trudeau
July, 1968

ANDY DONATO
THE TORONTO SUN, JULY 5, 1981

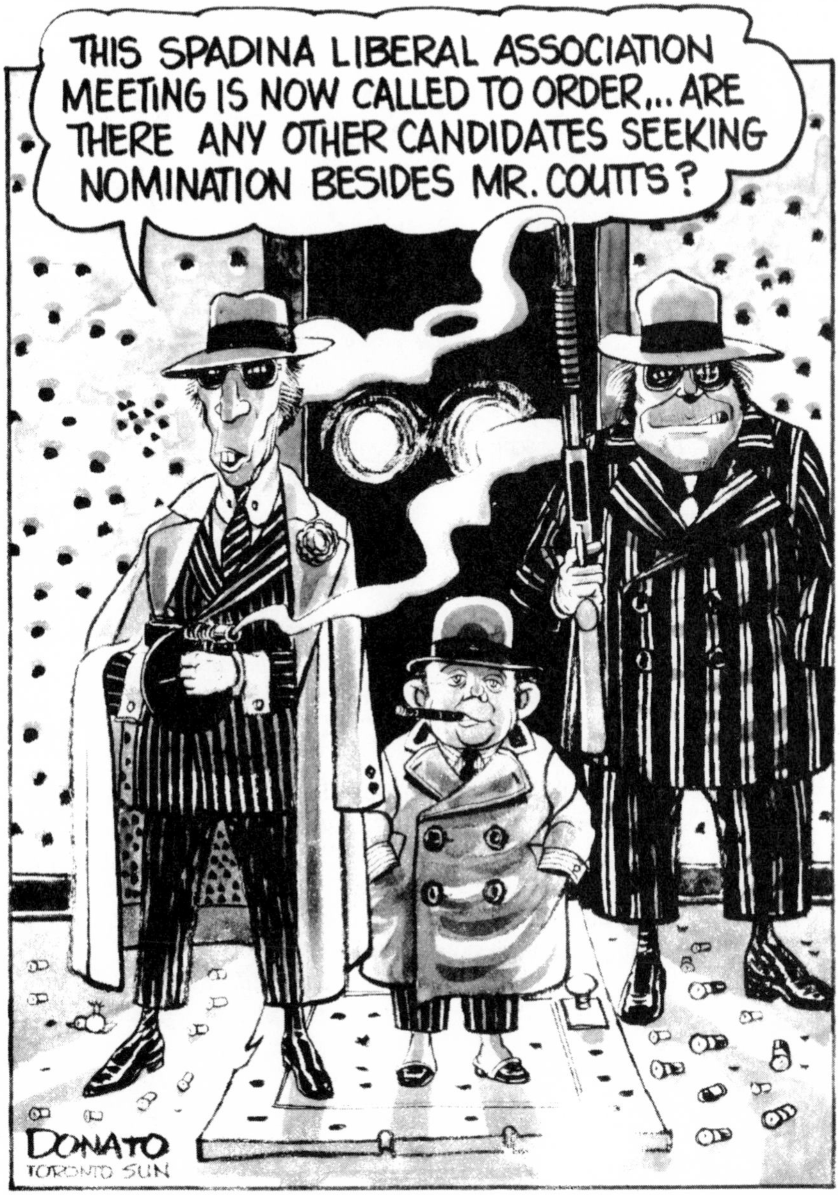
THIS SPADINA LIBERAL ASSOCIATION MEETING IS NOW CALLED TO ORDER,... ARE THERE ANY OTHER CANDIDATES SEEKING NOMINATION BESIDES MR. COUTTS?
DONATO
TORONTO SUN

"When (Tom) Axworthy wrote a letter to a friend in Paris prior to the May, 1979 election, he began his description of the Grits' predicament with the line 'Greetings from Custer's Last Stand!'"

—Christina McCall Newman
Grits

"The troops will need nerves of steel."
—Pierre Elliott Trudeau
speaking before calling the 1979 election
from Grits by Christina McCall Newman

"Be of good cheer, and don't be sad."
—Pierre Elliott Trudeau
speaking to supporters after May, 1979 defeat

"With all its sham, drudgery and broken dreams, it's still a beautiful world."
—Pierre Elliott
Trudeau quoting from Desiderata
May 23, 1979

"Trudeau, however, remained in his seat for about ten seconds while those around him stood and headed for the door. His head rested on his hand and his shoulders were hunched forward. Throughout the roll call vote, he had gazed downward, lifting his head only to listen to Clark's announcement. Then he dropped his head again and kept it there. When he looked up again, he had a quizzical, thin smile on his face."

—Jeffrey Simpson commenting
on the fall of the Clark government
from Discipline of Power

"If I hadn't had eight months in opposition, I don't think I would be feeling healthy and ready for a fight on the constitution or energy or on the economy after I had been elected."
—Pierre Elliott Trudeau,
interview with David Frost
February, 1982

AISLIN
MONTREAL GAZETTE, OCTOBER 18, 1979

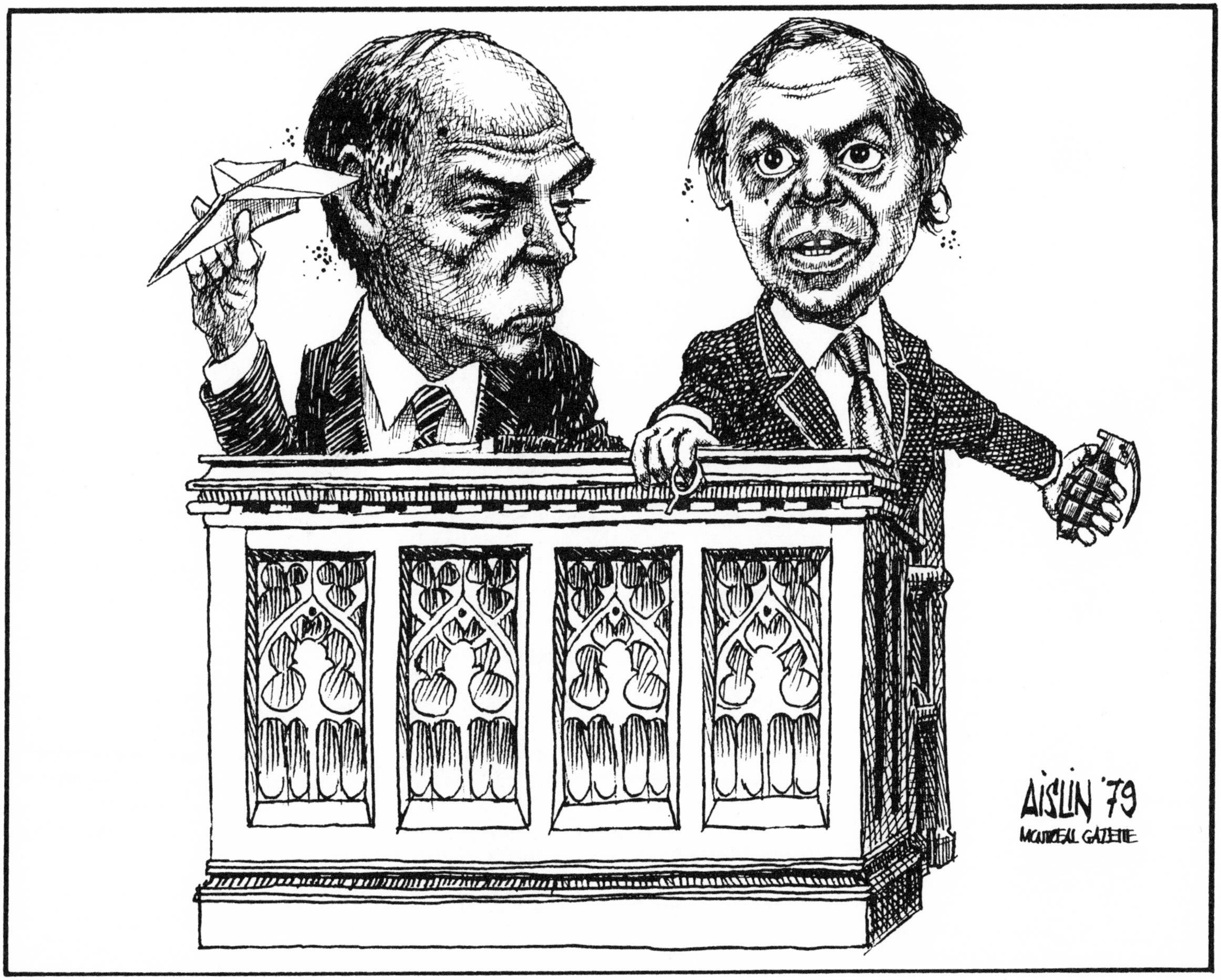
AISLIN '79
MONTREAL GAZETTE

"I have accepted the strong appeal of the National Liberal Caucus and the National Liberal Executive and I will lead our party in the current election campaign. If we are elected, I will form a new Liberal Government to govern our country.

"This was the single most difficult decision I have ever made. You know my reasons for wanting to step down from public life. My strongest desire was to leave politics and raise my family in Montreal.

"I decided last night, after two days of long consultation with friends and colleagues in the caucus and the party, that because Canada faces most serious problems, because the Government has been defeated and because our party faces an election, my duty is to accept the draft of my party — that duty was stronger even than my desire to continue with my plan to re-enter private life."

—Pierre Elliott Trudeau
December 17, 1979

EDD ULUSCHAK
EDMONTON JOURNAL, JANUARY 7, 1980

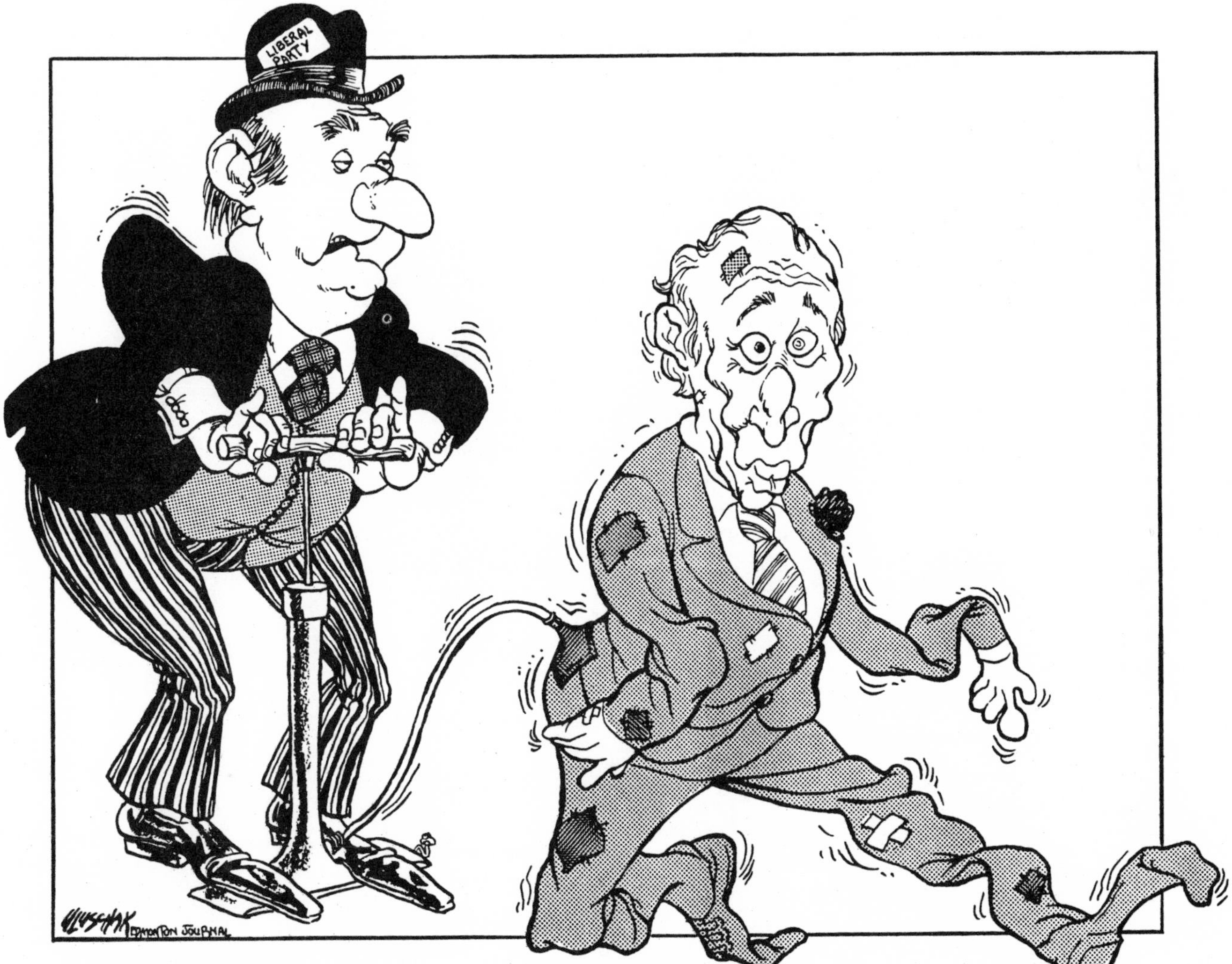
LIBERAL PARTY
EDMONTON JOURNAL

"Just one more time, Pierre."

"The powers of the national government
come to it under the constitution... and they
come from the people of Canada. And the
people of Canada want to vote in this election
to say clearly that they want a government
which will govern for the whole country, not
for one province against the others, not for one
part against the other."
 —*Pierre Elliott Trudeau, February 13, 1980*
 from Discipline of Power *by Jeffrey Simpson*

AISLIN
MONTREAL GAZETTE, FEBRUARY 7, 1980

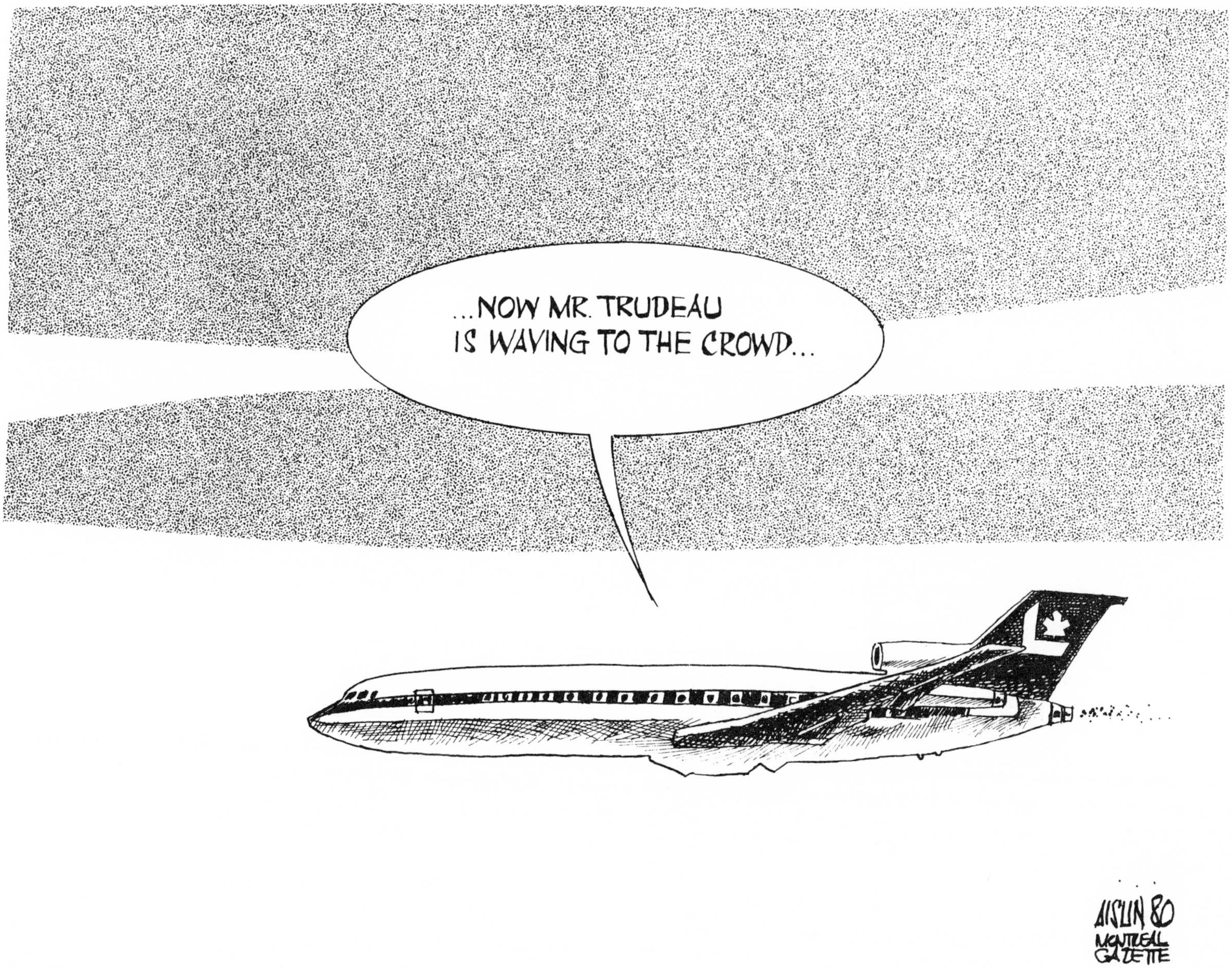
...NOW MR. TRUDEAU
IS WAVING TO THE CROWD...
AISLIN 80
MONTREAL
GAZETTE

"[Trudeau] is the only political leader in the history of this country, probably in the history of the world, whose slogan has been 'Elect me and I will quit.'"

—Joe Clark, January 8, 1980
from Discipline of Power *by Jeffrey Simpson*

"This sequence of events was so improbable that it bordered on the miraculous... Within a few months, Trudeau was Prime Minister again. Victory seemed to bring new energy and purpose. A few more months and he was focusing his efforts and our attention on a task that had baffled him for fifteen years and frustrated Canadian politicians for more than fifty: reforming the constitution and bringing it home. He was within sight of an achievement that would ensure his place in Canadian history."

—Peter Desbarats
Canada Lost Canada Found.

"'Welcome to the eighties,' the man said— his first words to the country on the night of his return from limbo, some ten months ago. P.E. Trudeau greeted the new decade with all the relish of a miraculous survivor who had enjoyed the luck of falling from his office window and landing on Joe Clark."

—Dalton Camp, December 26, 1980
An Eclectic Eel

"It is a joy to cook in the kitchen at 24 Sussex Dr., (Chef Yannick) Vincent says, because Prime Minister Pierre Trudeau is a connoisseur of food who really appreciates his efforts.

"Vincent lists calves' brains, piperade, veal kidney, snails and salmon among the Prime Minister's favorites."

—Mary McGrath, The Toronto Star
February 16, 1983

AISLIN
MONTREAL GAZETTE, FEBRUARY 18, 1980

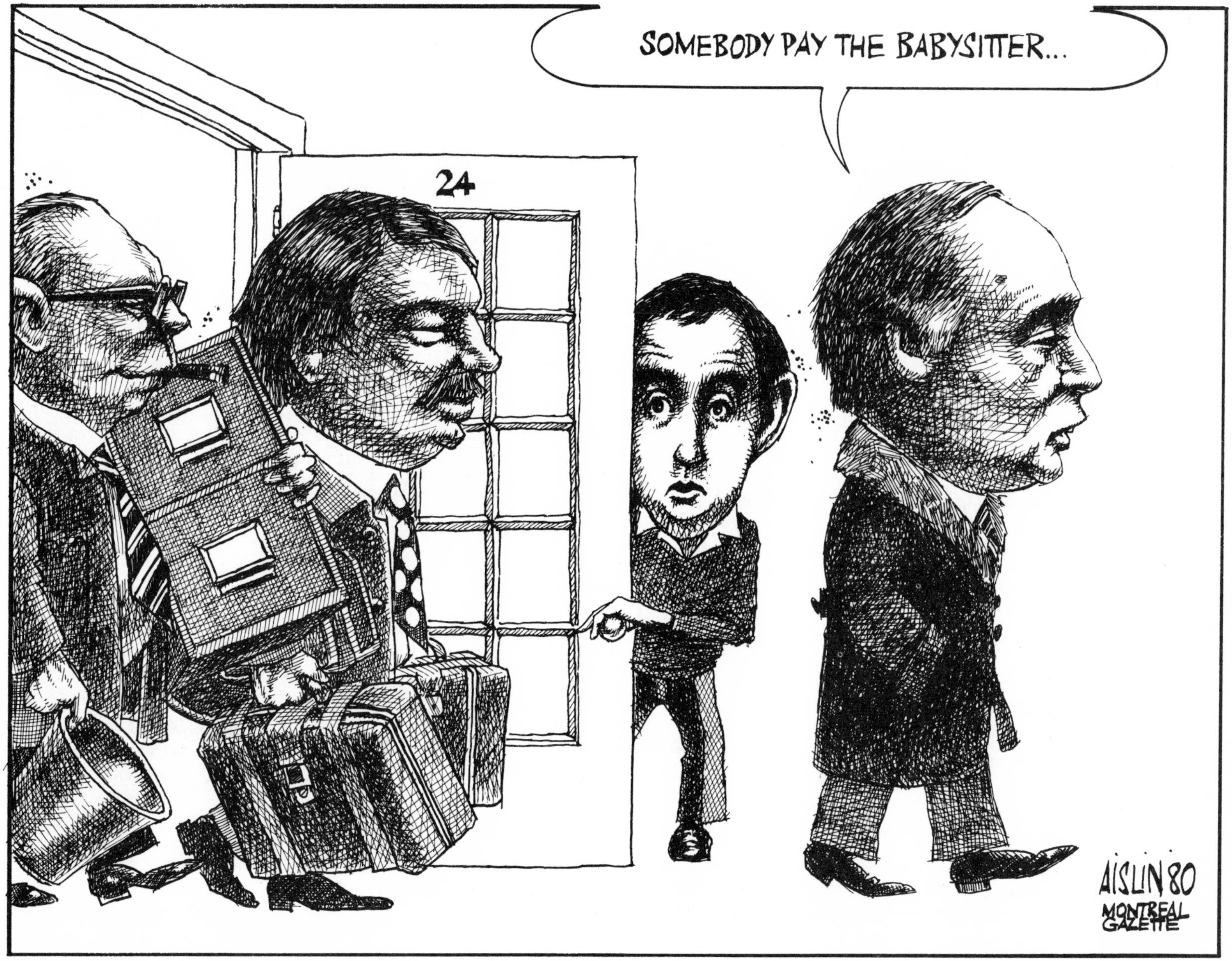
SOMEBODY PAY THE BABYSITTER...
24
AISLIN 80
MONTREAL GAZETTE

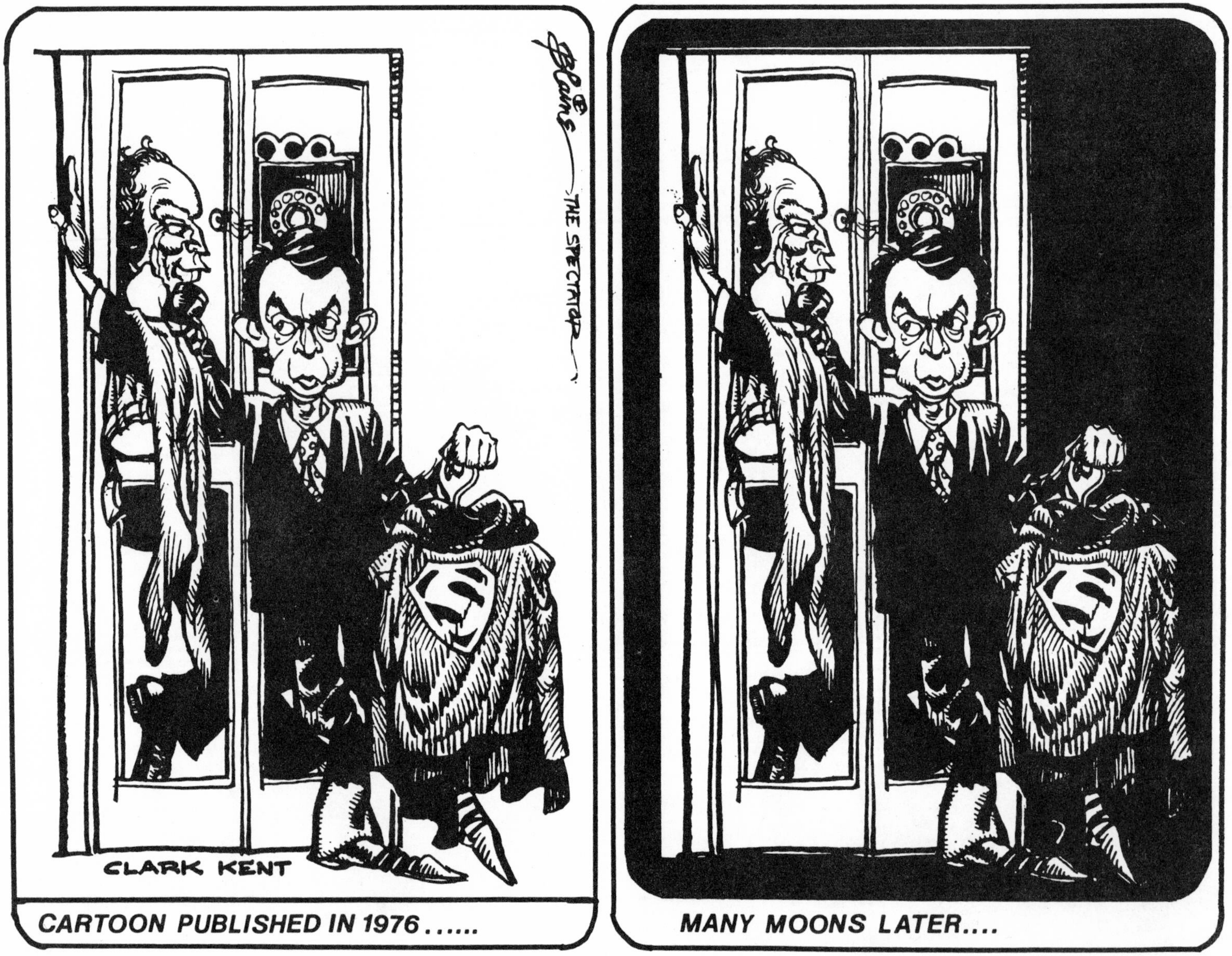
Blaine ©
THE SPECTATOR
CLARK KENT
CARTOON PUBLISHED IN 1976......
MANY MOONS LATER....

BLAINE
THE HAMILTON SPECTATOR, JANUARY 10, 1983

"Trudeau is a superb actor. Clark is a lousy one."

—Allan Fotheringham
Malice in Blunderland

"Clark struggled against Trudeau in Quebec like a heretic denouncing the Pope."

—Jeffrey Simpson commenting on the 1979-1980 election campaign in Discipline of Power

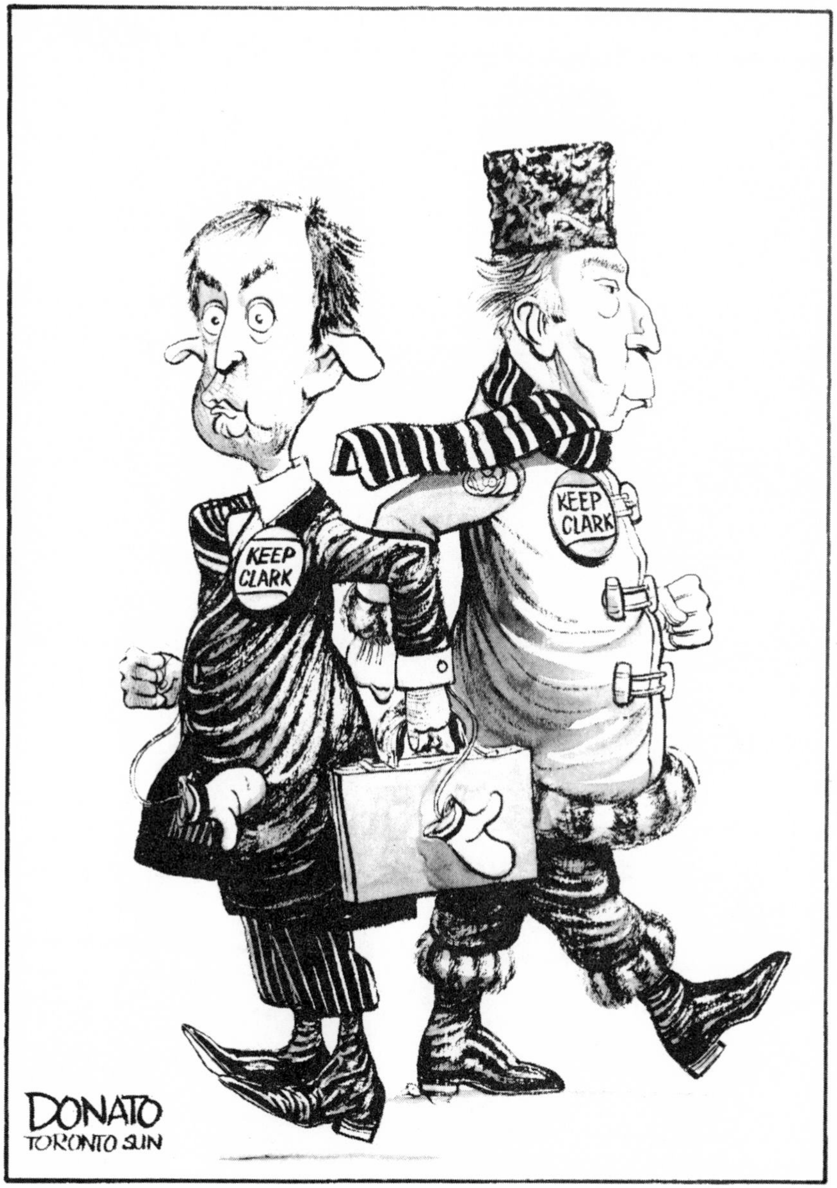
KEEP CLARK
KEEP CLARK
DONATO
TORONTO SUN

ANDY DONATO
THE TORONTO SUN, JANUARY 4, 1981

"Observing P.E. Trudeau, I sometimes think there are seven of him, one for every day of the week."

—Dalton Camp, November 1, 1979
from An Eclectic Eeel

"Somebody's going to say someday, 'Will the real Mr. Trudeau please stand up,' and about fifty-eight people will rise."

—An official at Liberal Party Headquarters
quoted by Edith Iglauer

Pierre Absolutely Trendy
Pierre Elliott Reincarnation
Pierre Easily Trendeau

—Nicknames applied by Allan Fotheringham

MIKE GRASTON
THE WINDSOR STAR, FEBRUARY 7, 1983

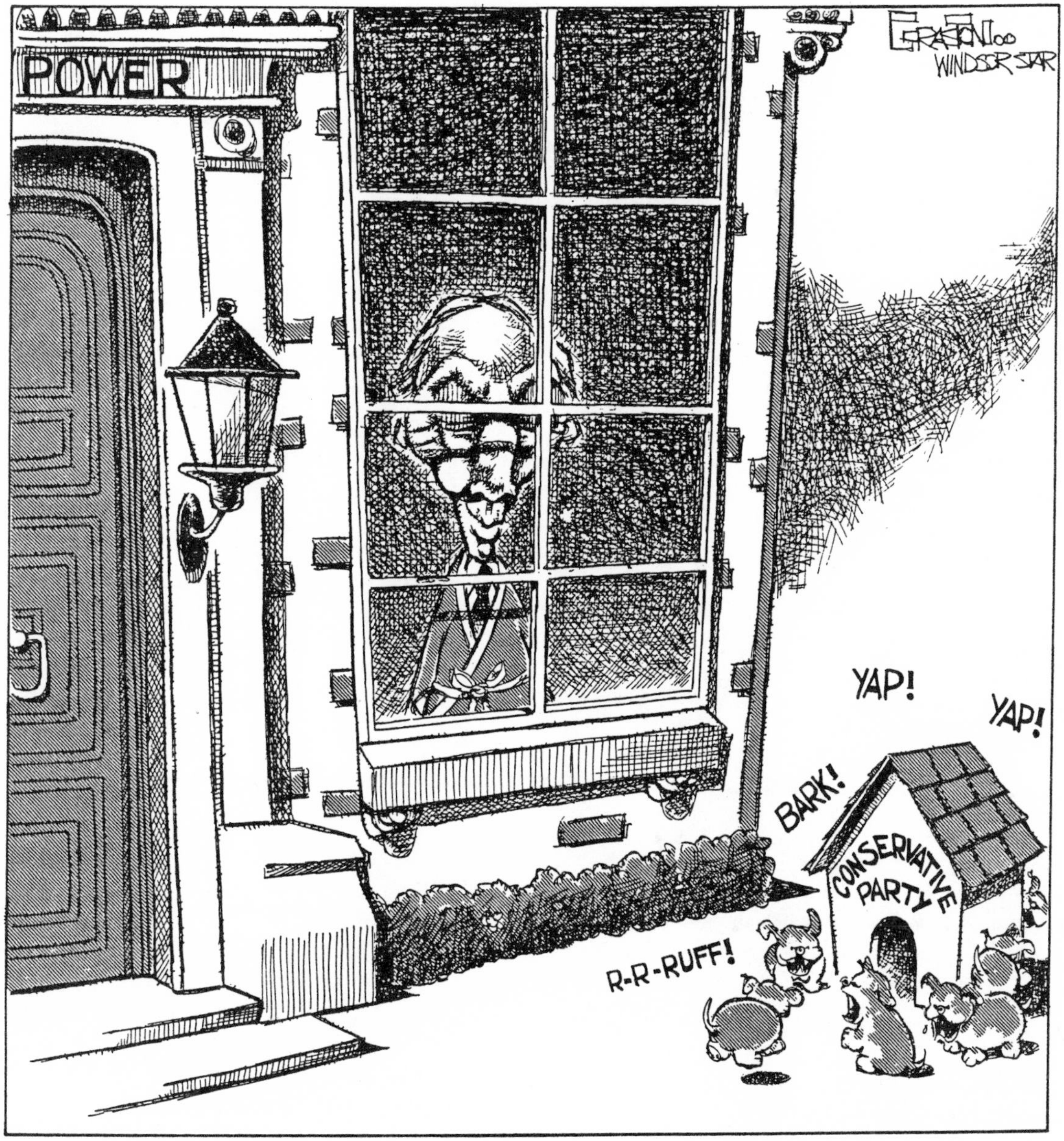
POWER
YAP!
YAP!
BARK!
CONSERVATIVE PARTY
R-R-RUFF!
WINDSOR STAR

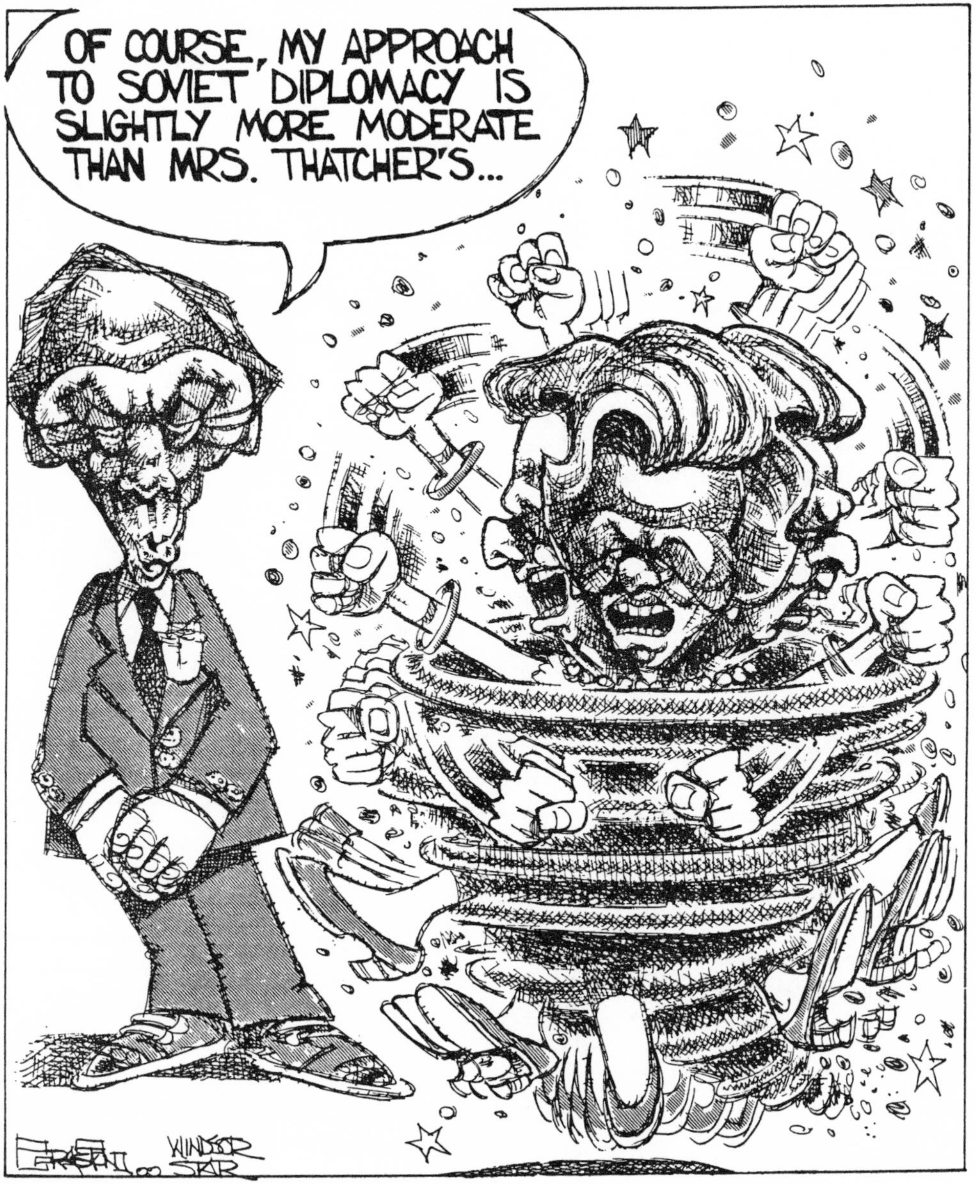
OF COURSE, MY APPROACH TO SOVIET DIPLOMACY IS SLIGHTLY MORE MODERATE THAN MRS. THATCHER'S...
WINDSOR STAR

THE WORLD

MIKE GRASTON
THE WINDSOR STAR, OCTOBER 3, 1983

"Unlike the Warsaw Pact, it is not sufficient for us as government leaders to merely proclaim our support for NATO. We must be able as well to persuade our electorates of the benefits of the alliance if we are not to be swept out of office or forced to change our policies."
—Pierre Elliott Trudeau
speaking at a NATO summit meeting,
May 30, 1975 from Pierre Elliott Trudeau
by Charles Bordeleau

"...Canadians look upon NATO as the cornerstone of our defence policy. We do not wish to be silent partners, however. It is a political alliance, after all, and politicians like to discuss and even argue the issues. If we disagree from time to time, and expend great effort in trying to resolve our differences, that is not a sign of weakness in the Alliance, but a sign of the strength which pervades a free association of independent countries."
—Pierre Elliott Trudeau
February 9, 1984

DUNCAN MACPHERSON
THE TORONTO STAR, NOVEMBER 15, 1968

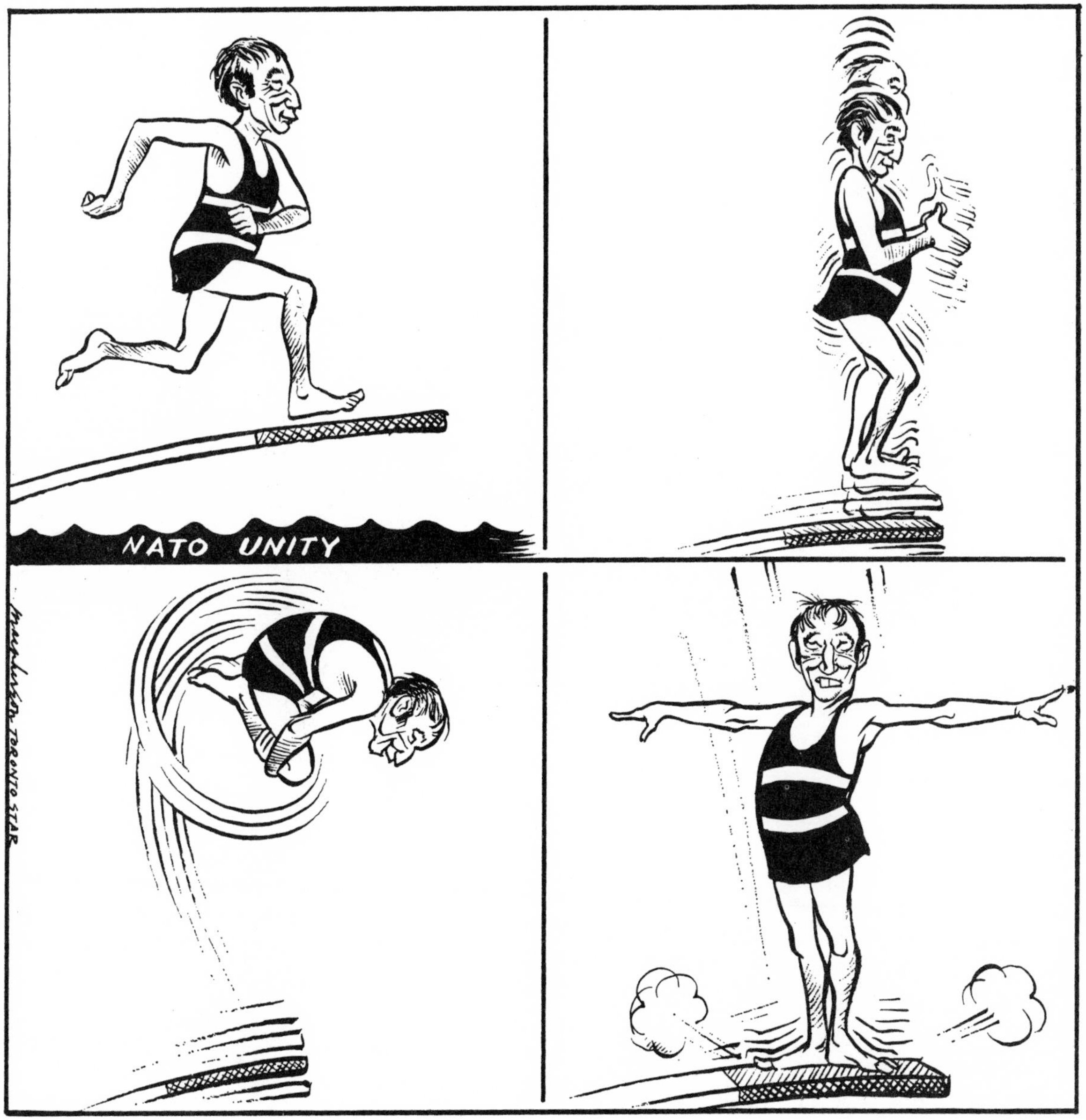
NATO UNITY
Macpherson TORONTO STAR

"Pierre Elliot Trudeau, the Prime Minister of Canada, arrives in Peking today for an official visit to our country at the invitation of the government of the People's Republic of China. The distinguished Canadian guest comes to China from far away, bringing with him friendship of the people of Canada. The people of China wish to extend a warm welcome to the distinguished guest."

Editorial
The People's Daily, *Peking*
October 9, 1973

"China is a country on the march."
—*Pierre Elliott Trudeau and Jacques Hebert*
Two Innocents in Red China

"When Trudeau went to China as a private citizen in 1960, he saw the future."
—*Philip C. Bom*
Trudeau's Canada

"I, personally, am not of the philosophy that because you extend bonds of friendship or of goodwill towards another country you are automatically taking it away from somebody else. This is not my vision of relations between human beings in society and it's not my view of the world."

—*Pierre Elliot Trudeau*
November 11, 1971

DUNCAN MACPHERSON
THE TORONTO STAR, DECEMBER 19, 1968

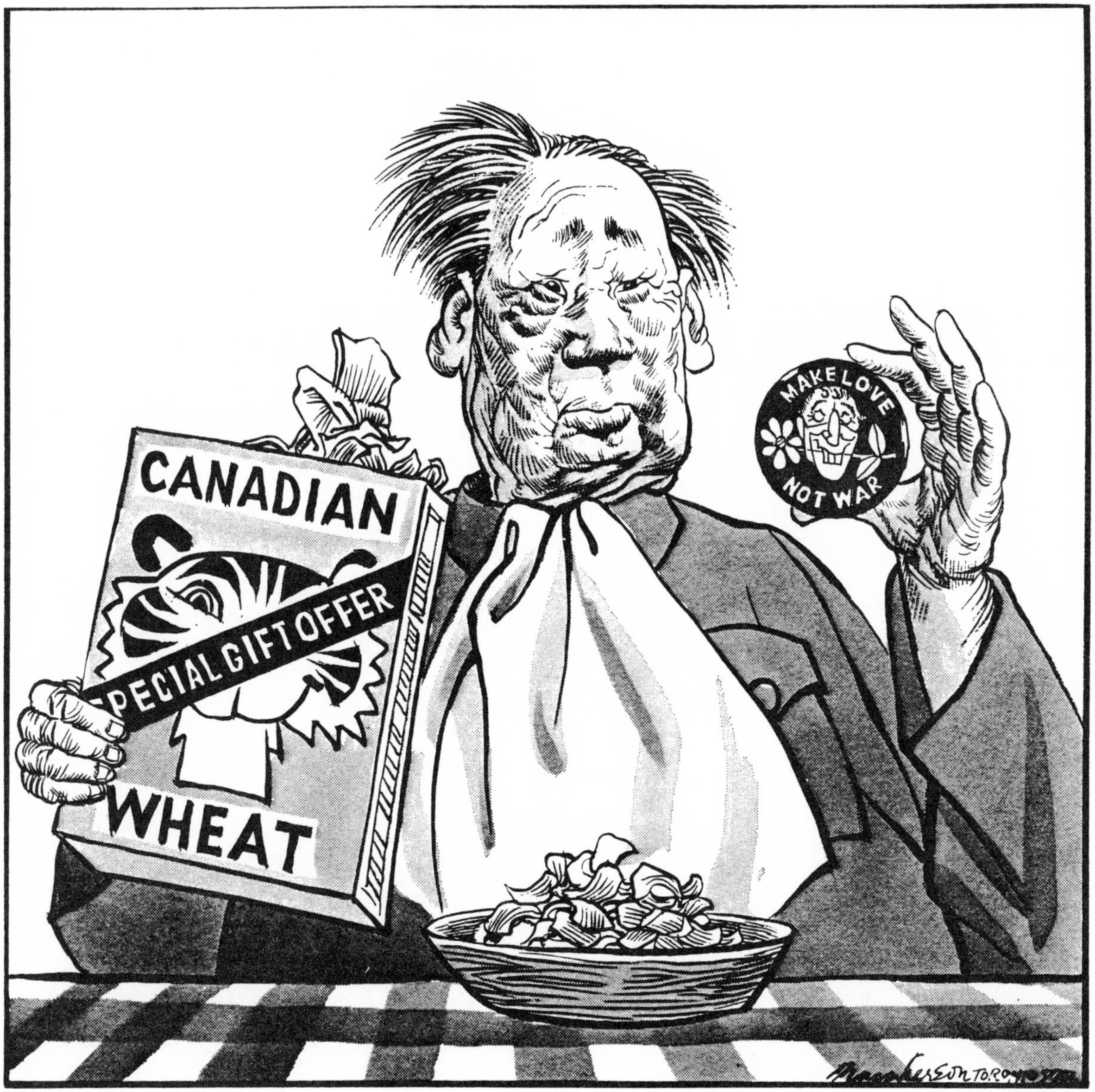
CANADIAN
SPECIAL GIFT OFFER
WHEAT
MAKE LOVE
NOT WAR

"A billion box tops and you get a free embassy."

"Canada is a country whose main exports are
hockey players and cold fronts. Our main
imports are baseball players and acid rain."
—*Pierre Elliot Trudeau
speaking to a Baseball All-Star Game luncheon,
July 13, 1982*

*DUNCAN MACPHERSON
THE TORONTO STAR, DECEMBER 2, 1971*

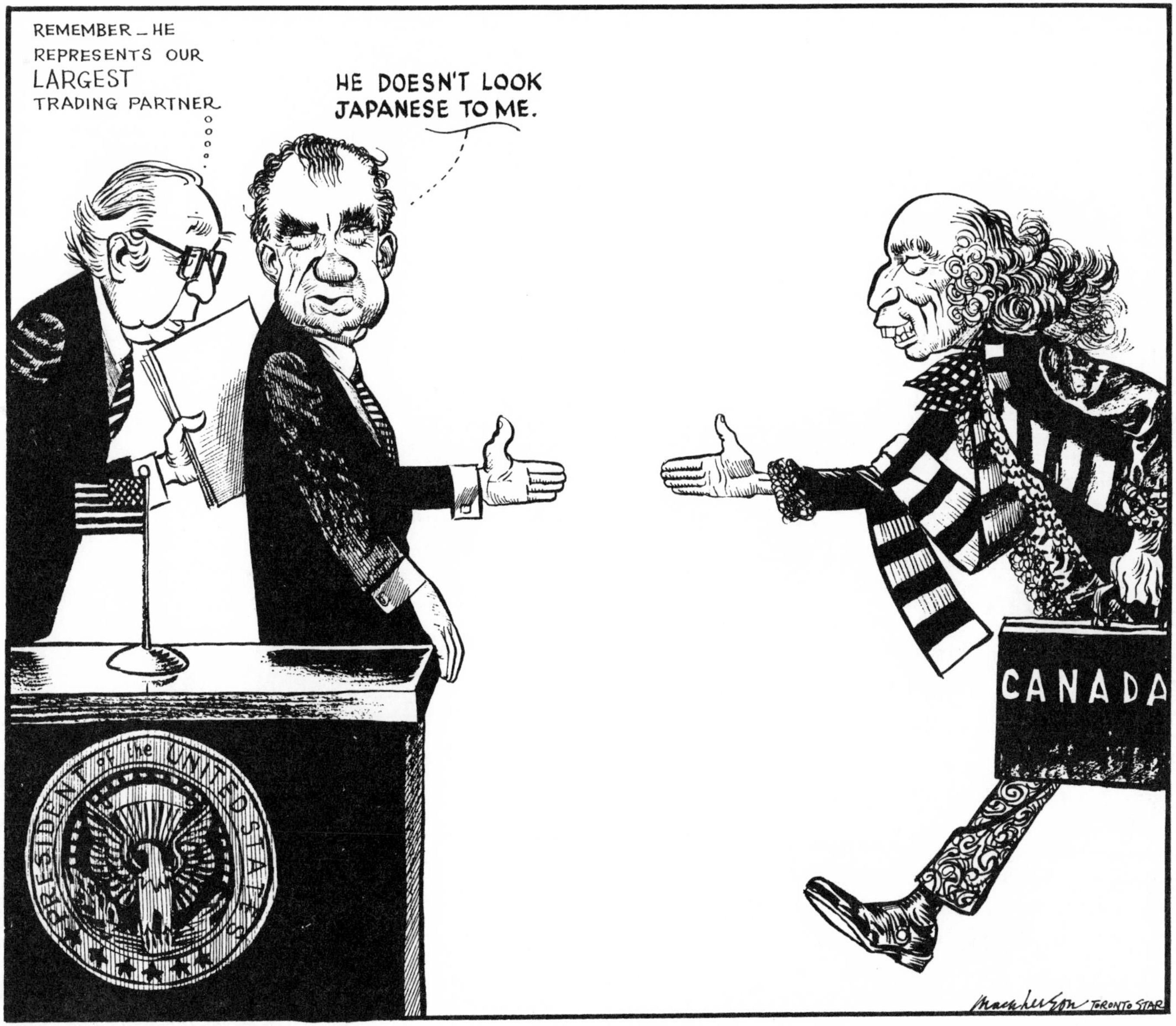
REMEMBER _ HE REPRESENTS OUR LARGEST TRADING PARTNER
HE DOESN'T LOOK JAPANESE TO ME.
PRESIDENT of the UNITED STATES
CANADA
Macpherson TORONTO STAR

"Living next to you is in some ways like
sleeping with an elephant: No matter how
friendly and even-tempered the beast, one is
affected by every twitch and grunt."
—Pierre Elliott Trudeau speaking to the
Press Club in Washington, D.C.,
March 25, 1969 from Presidents and
Prime Ministers *by Lawrence Martin*

FRANKLIN
THE GLOBE AND MAIL, FEBRUARY 21, 1977

"Grits are very popular in the South, but I understand this isn't the case in your country."

"At times in our history we have paused to
wonder whether your friendly invitations to
'come and stay a while' have not been aimed at
Canada as a political unit rather than at
Canadians as individuals."
       —Pierre Elliott Trudeau speaking to the
       Press Club in Washington, D.C.,
       March 25, 1969 from
       Presidents and Prime Ministers
       by Lawrence Martin

ADRIAN RAESIDE
TIMES-COLONIST, MARCH 9, 1981

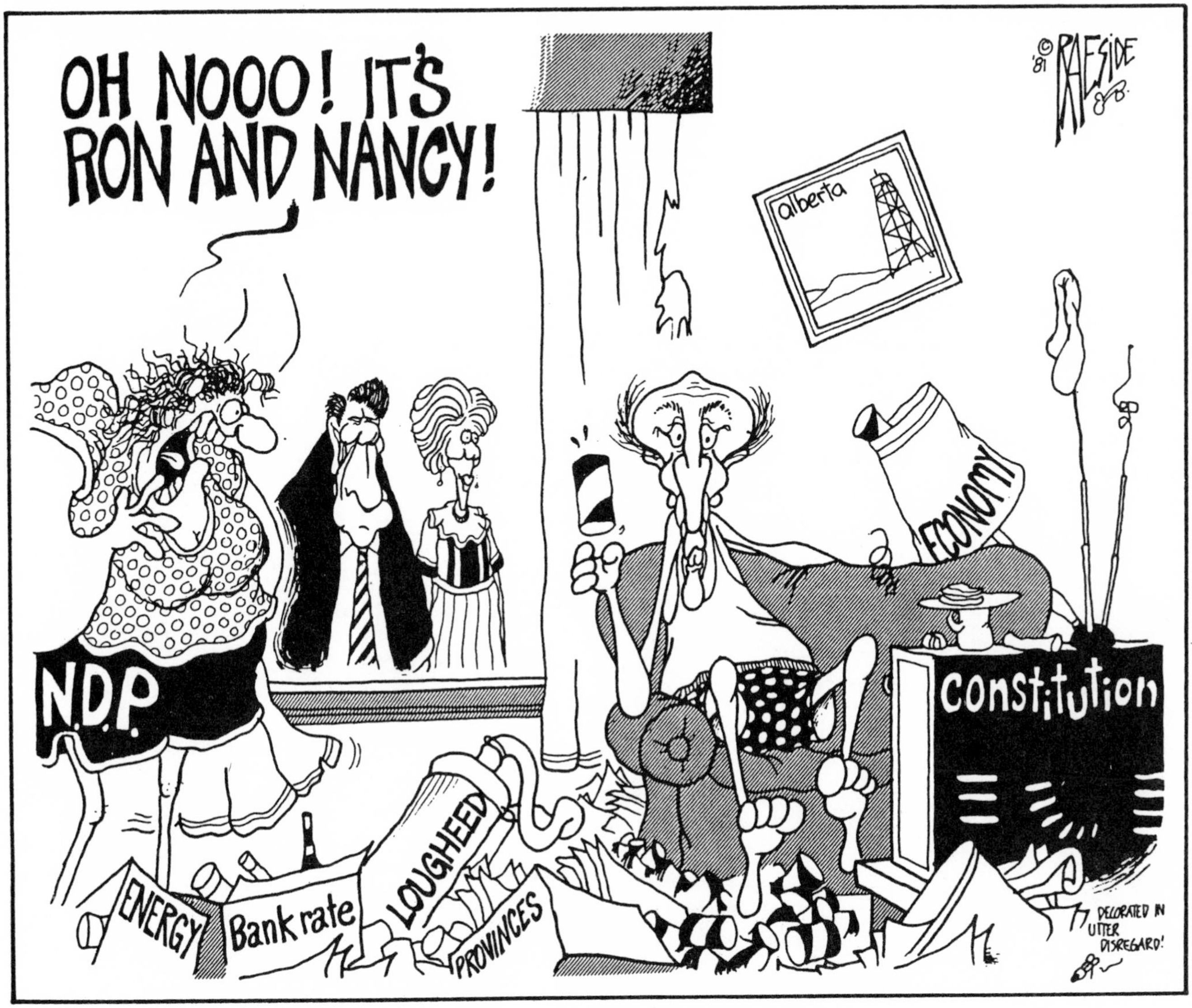
OH NOOO! IT'S RON AND NANCY!
©'81 RAESIDE
alberta
ECONOMY
N.D.P.
constitution
ENERGY
Bank rate
LOUGHEED
PROVINCES
DECORATED IN UTTER DISREGARD!

"In the cast of world leaders, few if any rival
Pierre Trudeau in terms of respect. His conceptual
view of world politics, his independence and
forthrightness, his intellectual breadth, his
incisive insights, his eloquence all have drawn
almost universal statements of admiration."
—Kenneth Freed
Los Angeles Times

ADRIAN RAESIDE
TIMES-COLONIST, MAY 31, 1983

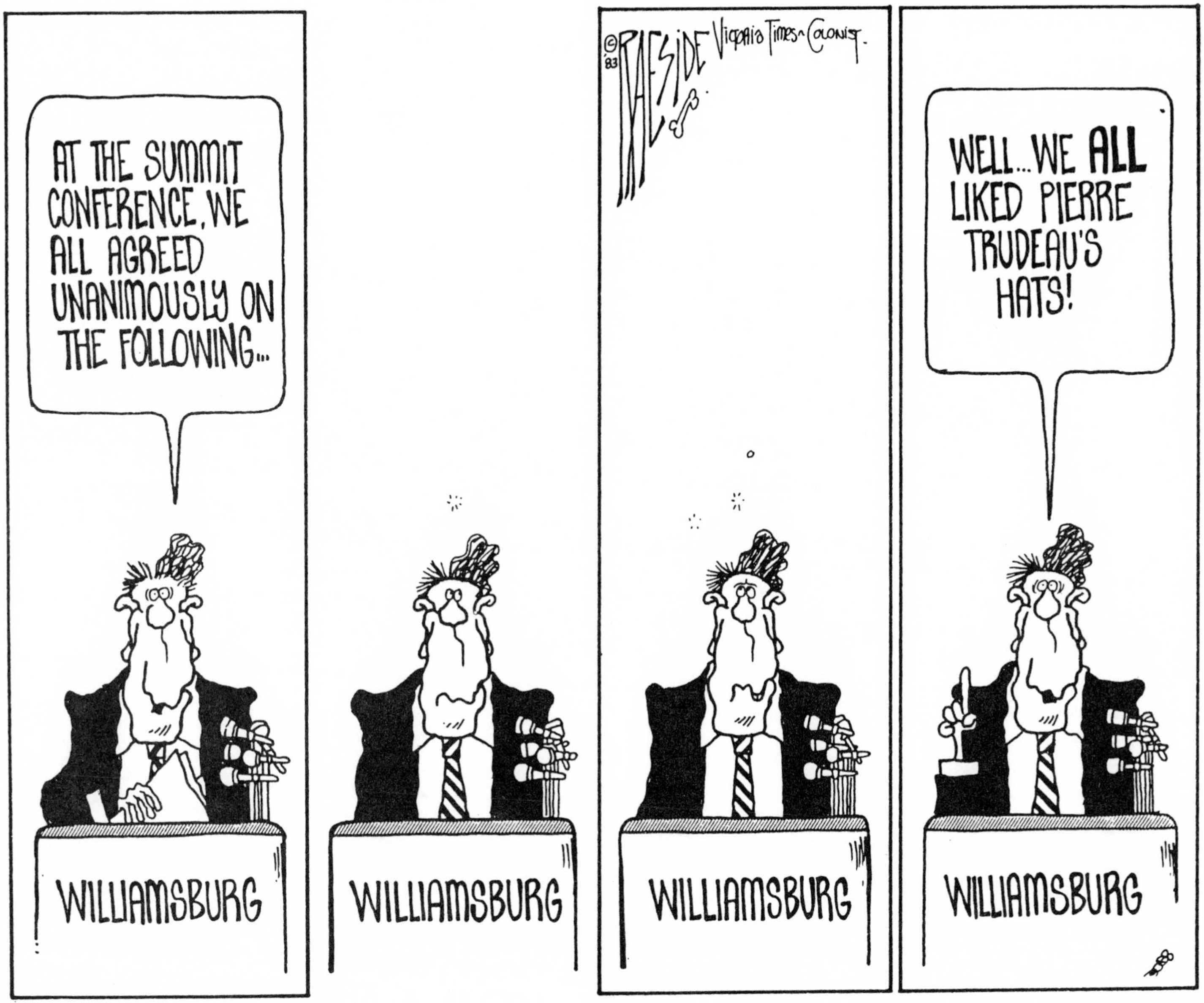
AT THE SUMMIT CONFERENCE, WE ALL AGREED UNANIMOUSLY ON THE FOLLOWING...
WILLIAMSBURG
WILLIAMSBURG
©'83 RAESIDE Victoria Times-Colonist
WILLIAMSBURG
WELL...WE ALL LIKED PIERRE TRUDEAU'S HATS!
WILLIAMSBURG

"Peace and security are not cold abstractions. Their purpose is to preserve the future of mankind, the growth of the human spirit, and the patrimony of our planet.

"The choice we face is clear and present. We can without effort abandon our fate to the mindless drift toward nuclear war. Or we can gather our strength, working in good company to turn aside the forces bearing down on us, on our children, on this Earth.

"As for me, I choose to move forward."

—Pierre Elliott Trudeau
November 13, 1983

"If our future depended on Canadians alone, we could be confident that it was safe and sound. But no nation today holds its future securely in its own hands. We share this planet with about 160 other nations, all of whom interact with us in a global system embracing our security, our economy, the health of our environment, and the quality of our lives."

—Pierre Elliott Trudeau
November 13, 1983

FRANK EDWARDS
THE WHIG-STANDARD, NOVEMBER 3, 1983

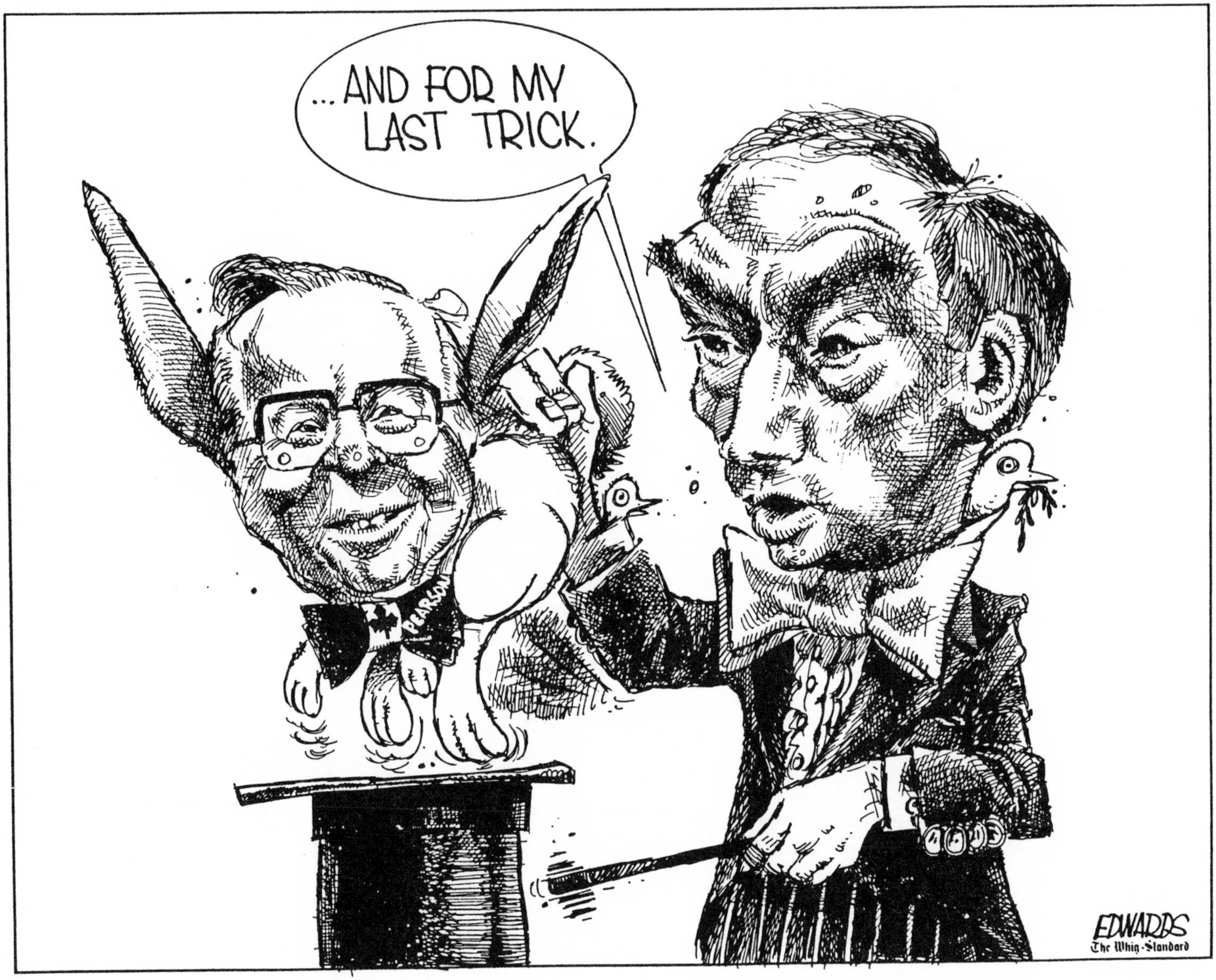
...AND FOR MY LAST TRICK.
PEARSON
EDWARDS
The Whig-Standard

"The people of Canada want peace. They don't care what the Pentagon says."

—Pierre Elliott Trudeau
December 13, 1983

"...in my day, I have been a Peacenik and in a sense a lot of my opponents in politics still think I am. You have heard people across the aisle of the House of Commons accuse me because I have been to the Soviet Union, or because I tried to say: 'Well, they are not such bad people and we should have treaties with them and so on.'

"So, in that role, I hope people would not say that I was a tool of the Soviet Union. I am trying to do what is best for Canada...

"...we knew after the Second World War that a lot of the peace movements were Communist fronts. That does not mean that the people who are seeking peace are Communist tools. I mean they are not acting, to help the Soviet Union, but that the Soviet Union uses them and the knowledge of their demonstrations on the checker board is obvious."

—Pierre Elliott Trudeau
May 14, 1983

"It is my personal purpose to live up to the undertaking, made by leaders at the Williamsburg Summit last May, 'to devote our full political resources to reducing the threat of war.' The questions to be raised...are not easy. There are priorities which inevitably conflict. A new climate of East-West confidence cannot be instilled in a day, nor can the arms race be stopped overnight. But insofar as I, and other leaders who share this purpose, can work together to build authentic confidence, I pledge to you that we shall."

—Pierre Elliott Trudeau
October 27, 1983

EDD ULUSCHAK
EDMONTON JOURNAL, DECEMBER 19, 1983

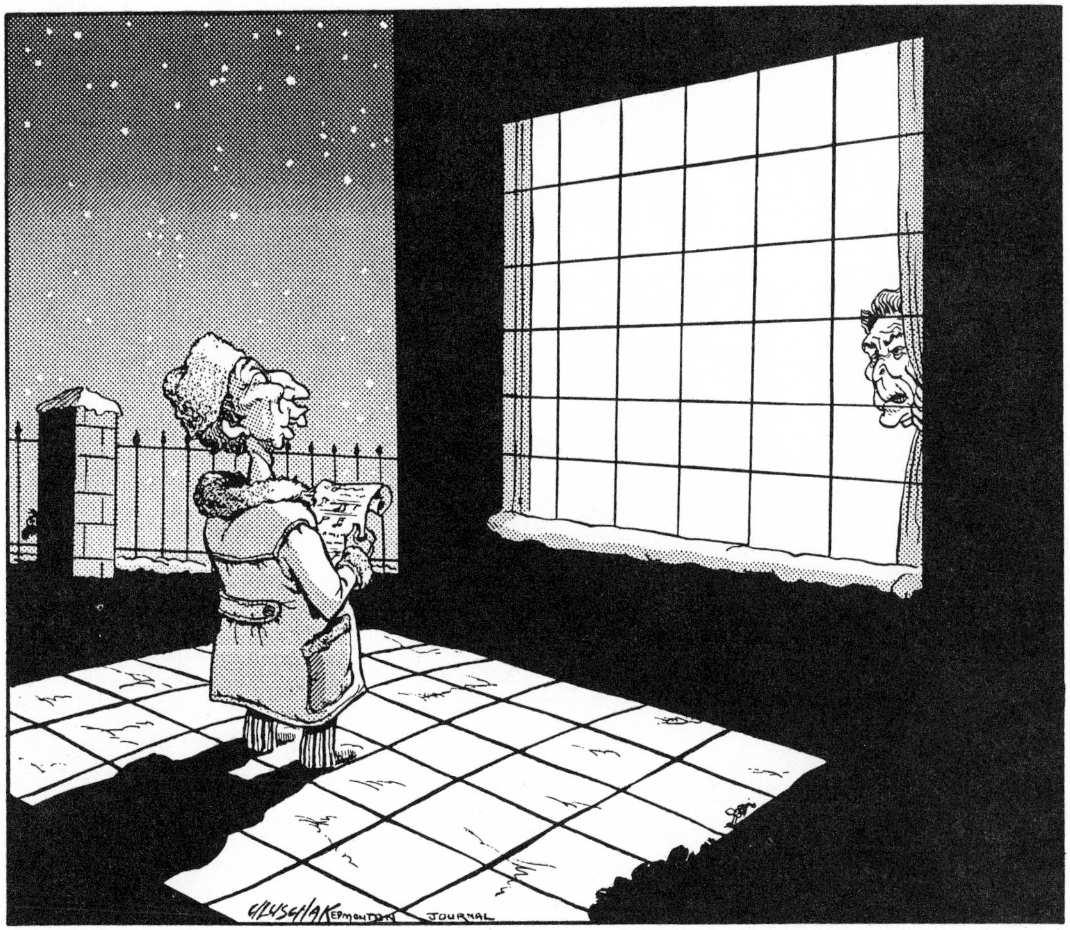
EDMONTON JOURNAL

"Get your pearl-handled gun, Nancy—it's one of those peaceniks singing carols on our lawn about peace on earth."

"...I see the two superpowers like two hockey teams. They are supposed to play a peaceful game, but sometimes a fight breaks out and one side begins to strike the other side and the other side strikes back. I suppose it is an academic question as to who strikes first. What is important is to stop the fighting and to get on with the game. That is what interests the Canadian people. They know that if a fight breaks out between the two superpowers, it will be different from a hockey game in that all the spectators will also be destroyed. So, we are like the spectators or the referees at a hockey match: We are telling the players to get back to the table, get back to the game."
—Pierre Elliott Trudeau
News conference, Prague, Czechoslovakia
January 26, 1984

"Action in the reduction of nuclear arms is, I repeat, something for which we are all, and must all, be striving.

"...nobody gave the superpowers the right to decide the future, the survival of humanity. In reality, if they don't make progress, if crisis becomes the current state of affairs, then the future of humanity is very much at stake and therefore we all have a right and a duty to be involved in that."
—Pierre Elliott Trudeau
January 28, 1984

"Nuclear weapons exist. They probably always will. And they work, with horrible efficiency. They threaten the very future of our species. We have no choice but to manage that risk. Never again can we put the task out of our minds; nor trivialize it; nor make it routine.

"Nor dare we lose heart."
—Pierre Elliott Trudeau
February 9, 1984

"And let it be said of Canada, and of Canadians: that we saw the crisis; that we did act; that we took risks; that we were loyal to our friends and open with our adversaries; that we lived up to our ideals; and that we have done what we could to lift the shadow of war."
—Pierre Elliott Trudeau
February 9, 1984

"The doomsday clock must stop at five minutes to 12:00."
—Pierre Elliott Trudeau
on the Korean airline disaster

FRANK EDWARDS
THE WHIG-STANDARD, OCTOBER 28, 1983

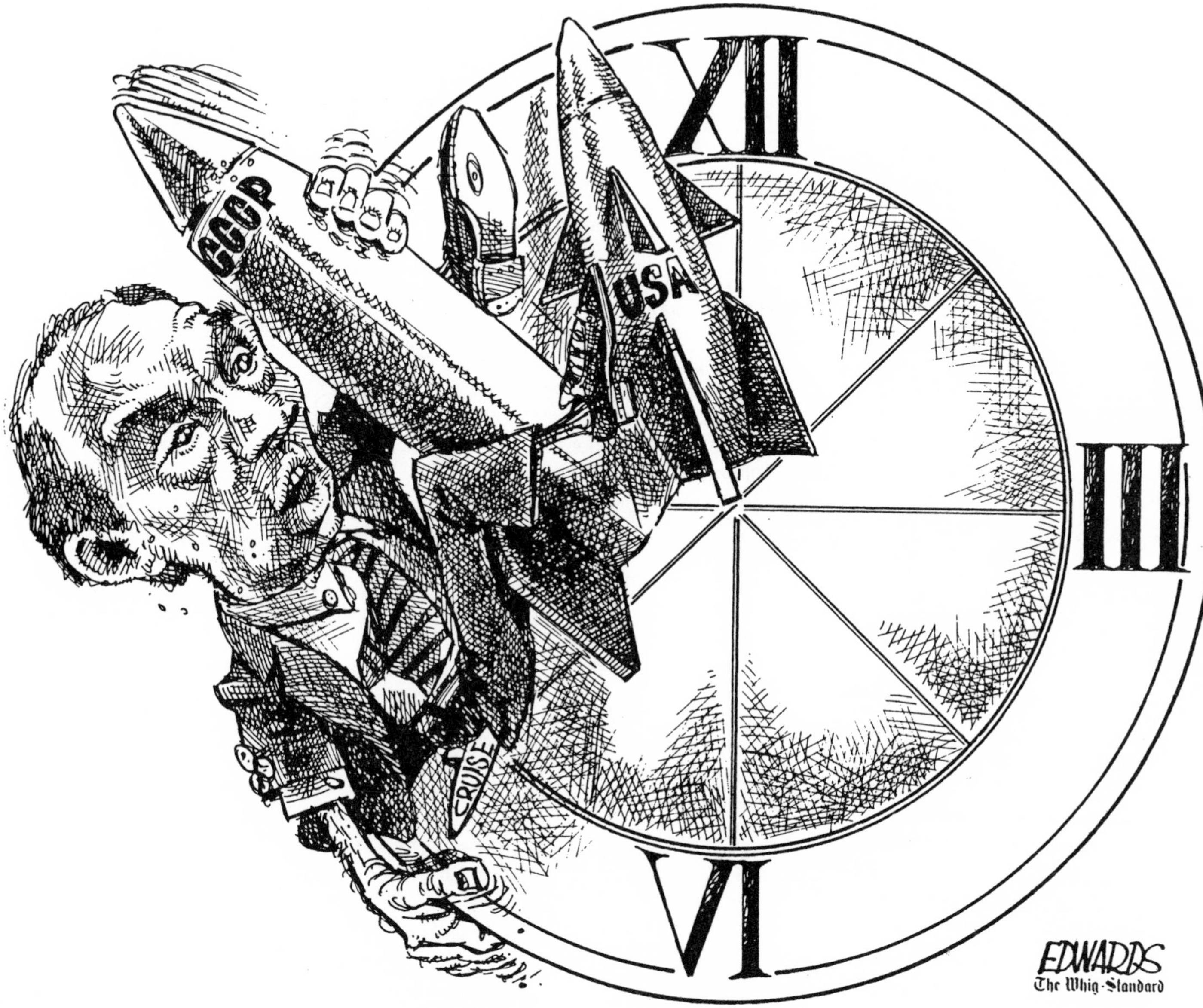
CCCP
USA
CRUISE
XII
III
VI
EDWARDS
The Whig-Standard

"Basically, once again, they, the cruise
protesters. are demonstrating against what
they see as the policy of an American president
who has rightly or wrongly been perceived as
warlike, or so hostile to the Soviet Union that
he cannot be trusted to look for peace. As I said
earlier, unfortunately President Reagan and
some of the people around him, have given
some justification for those fears."
—Pierre Elliott Trudeau
May 14, 1983

EDD ULUSCHAK
EDMONTON JOURNAL, MAY 27, 1983

CRUISE
EDMONTON JOURNAL
ULUSCHAK

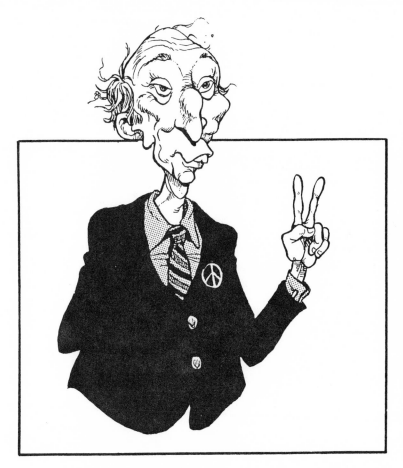

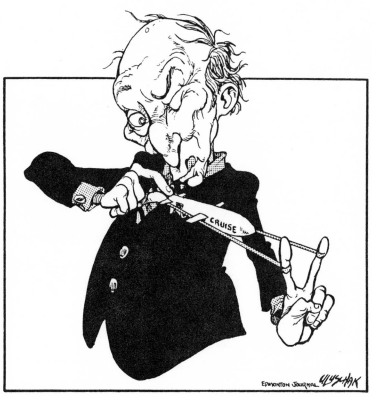

"It is hardly fair to rely on the Americans to protect the West, but to refuse to lend them a hand when the going gets rough. In that sense, the anti-Americanism of some Canadians verges on hypocrisy. They're eager to take refuge under the American umbrella, but don't want to help hold it."

—Pierre Elliott Trudeau
from an open letter to all Canadians
concerning cruise missile testing in Canada
May 9, 1983

"I think it, cruise testing. is a very important cause. I have been, in my day, in nuclear protests, too. I have written on it in *Cite Libre* and I have been pre-occupied with nuclear escalation and the possibility of nuclear war throughout my career, before being a prime minister and since being a prime minister.

"... I say 'some Canadians who protest against the United States verge on hypocrisy,' or words to that effect. It is obvious that in the thousands, and hundreds of thousands, of Canadians who are concerned about nuclear weapons, some are anti-American for the wrong reason."

—Pierre Elliott Trudeau
May 14, 1983

EDD ULUSCHAK
EDMONTON JOURNAL, NOVEMBER 2, 1983

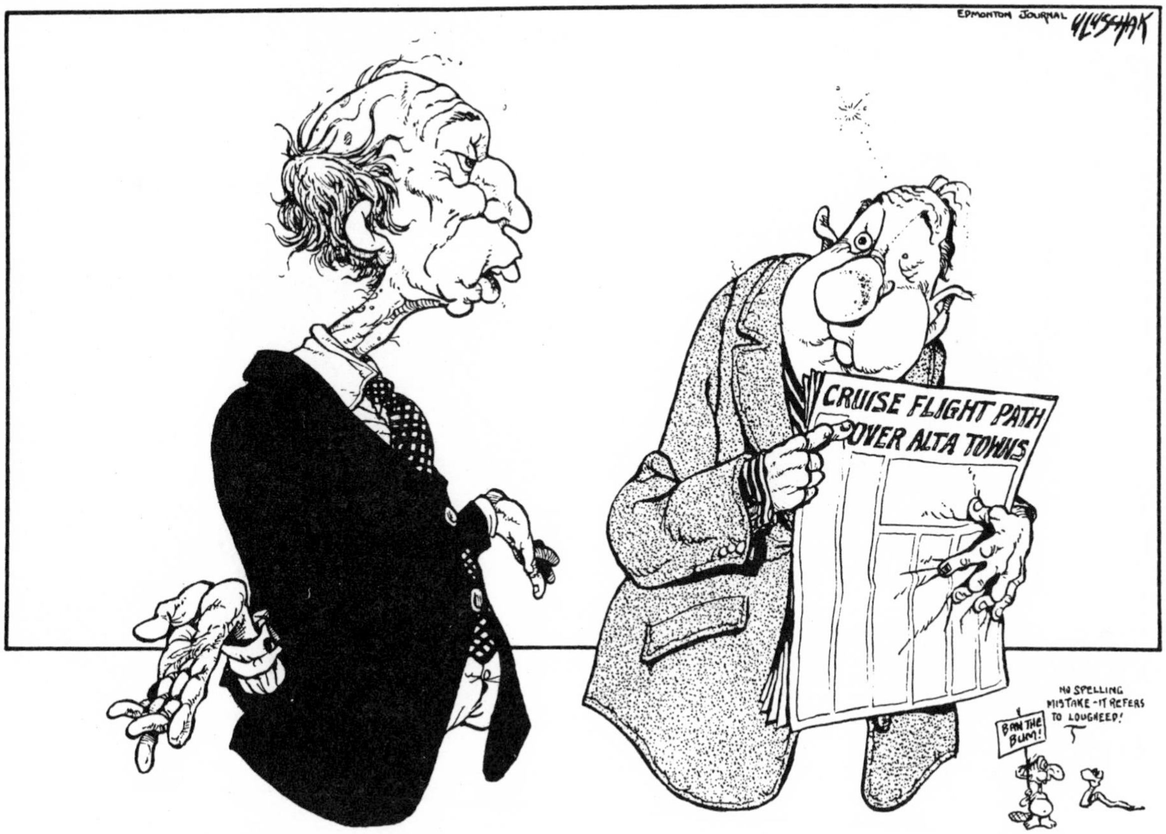
EDMONTON JOURNAL
ULUSCHAK
CRUISE FLIGHT PATH OVER ALTA TOWNS
BAN THE BUM!
NO SPELLING MISTAKE - IT REFERS TO LOUGHEED!

"So what's the fuss? Even if one crashes in a populated area, the chances of hitting a Liberal voter are nil!"

THE CONSTITUTION

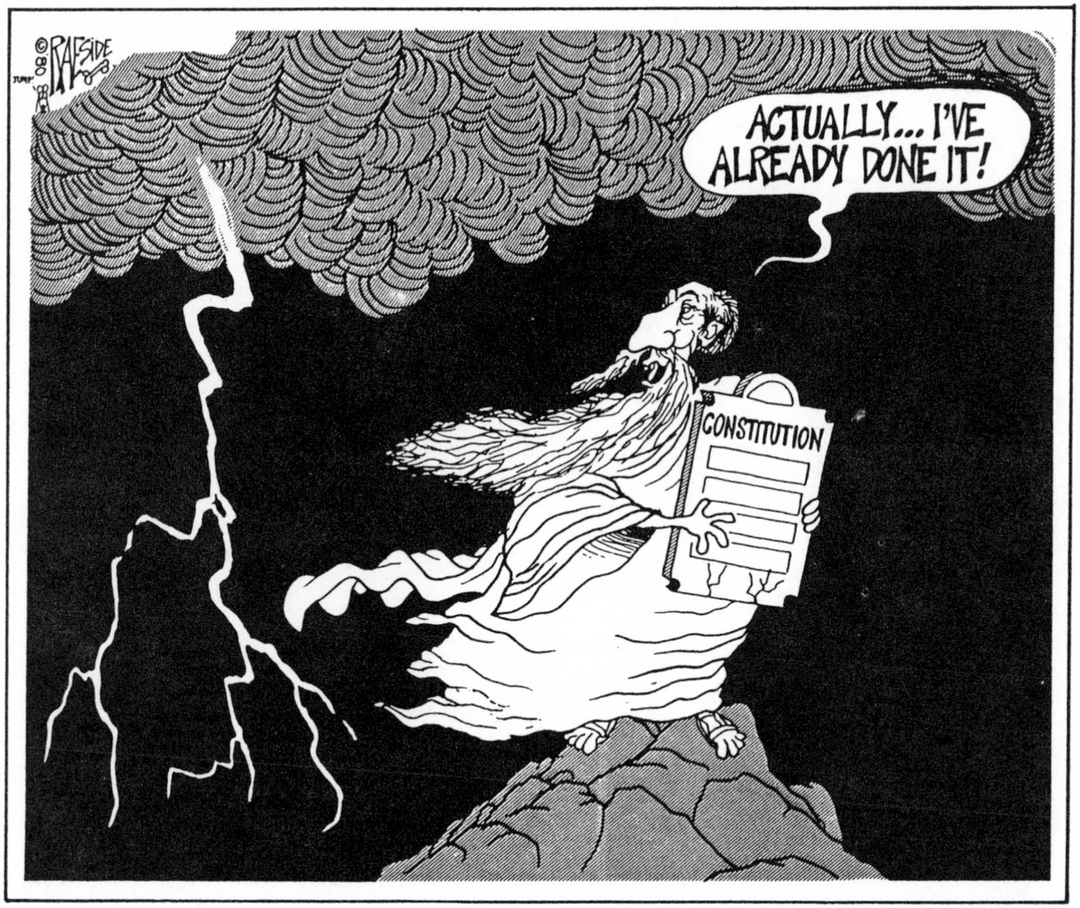

ACTUALLY... I'VE ALREADY DONE IT!
CONSTITUTION

ADRIAN RAESIDE
TIMES-COLONIST

"If Canada's strength is in her people, her vigour is in the future toward which Canadians have turned instinctively for centuries. I personally do not share with any acuteness the sense of regret expressed by some commentators that Canadians pay insufficient heed to their past. The past we must understand and respect, but it is not to be worshipped. It is in the future that we shall find our greatness."
—*Pierre Elliott Trudeau*
October 9, 1970

DUNCAN MACPHERSON
THE TORONTO STAR, SEPTEMBER 17, 1970

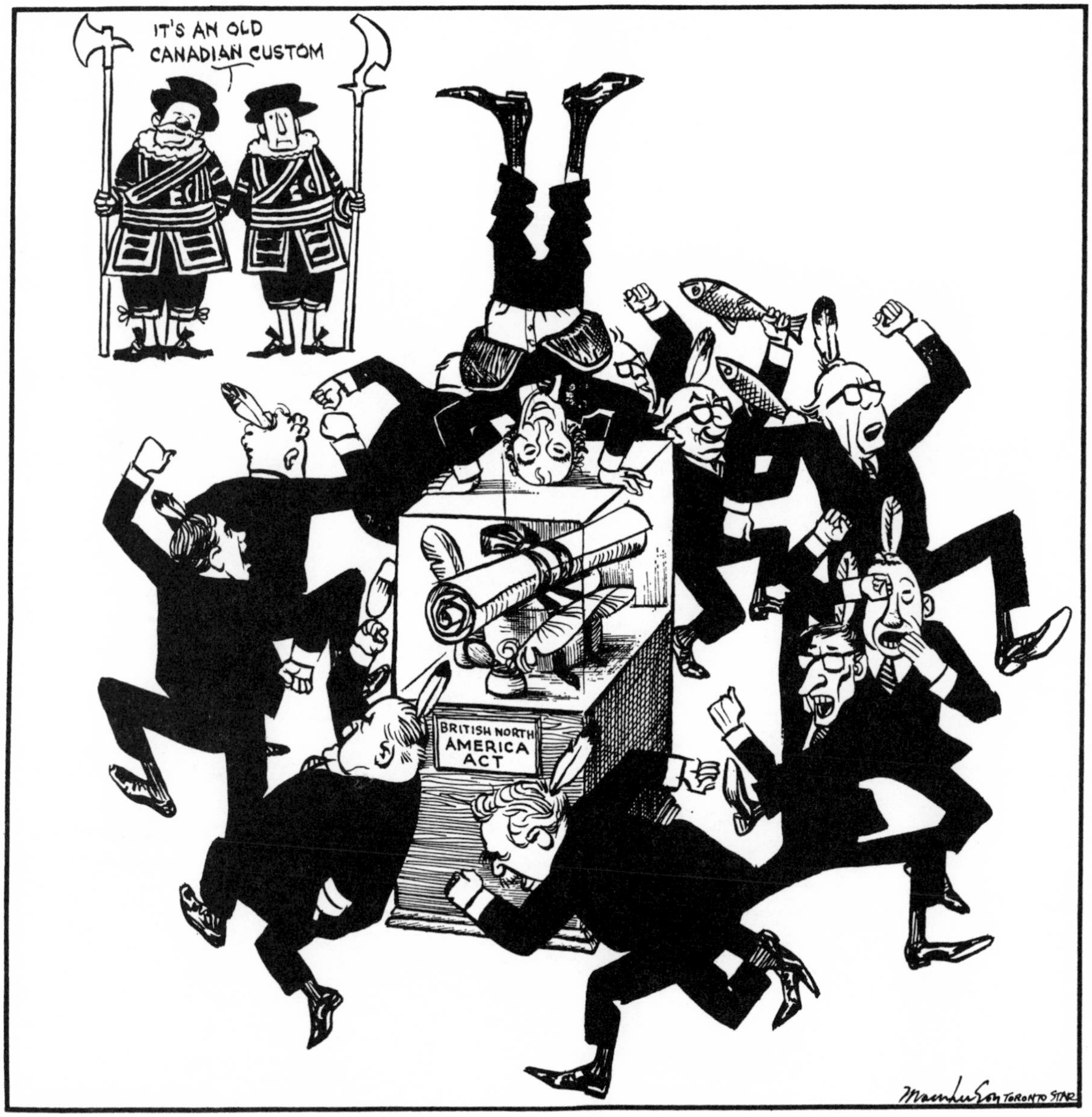
IT'S AN OLD CANADIAN CUSTOM
BRITISH NORTH AMERICA ACT
TORONTO STAR

Tower of London

"I am not in a frantic hurry to change the constitution simply because I am in a frantic hurry to change reality."
—*Pierre Elliott Trudeau*
from Trudeau's Canada *by Philip C. Bom*

FRANKLIN
THE GLOBE AND MAIL, APRIL 17, 1976

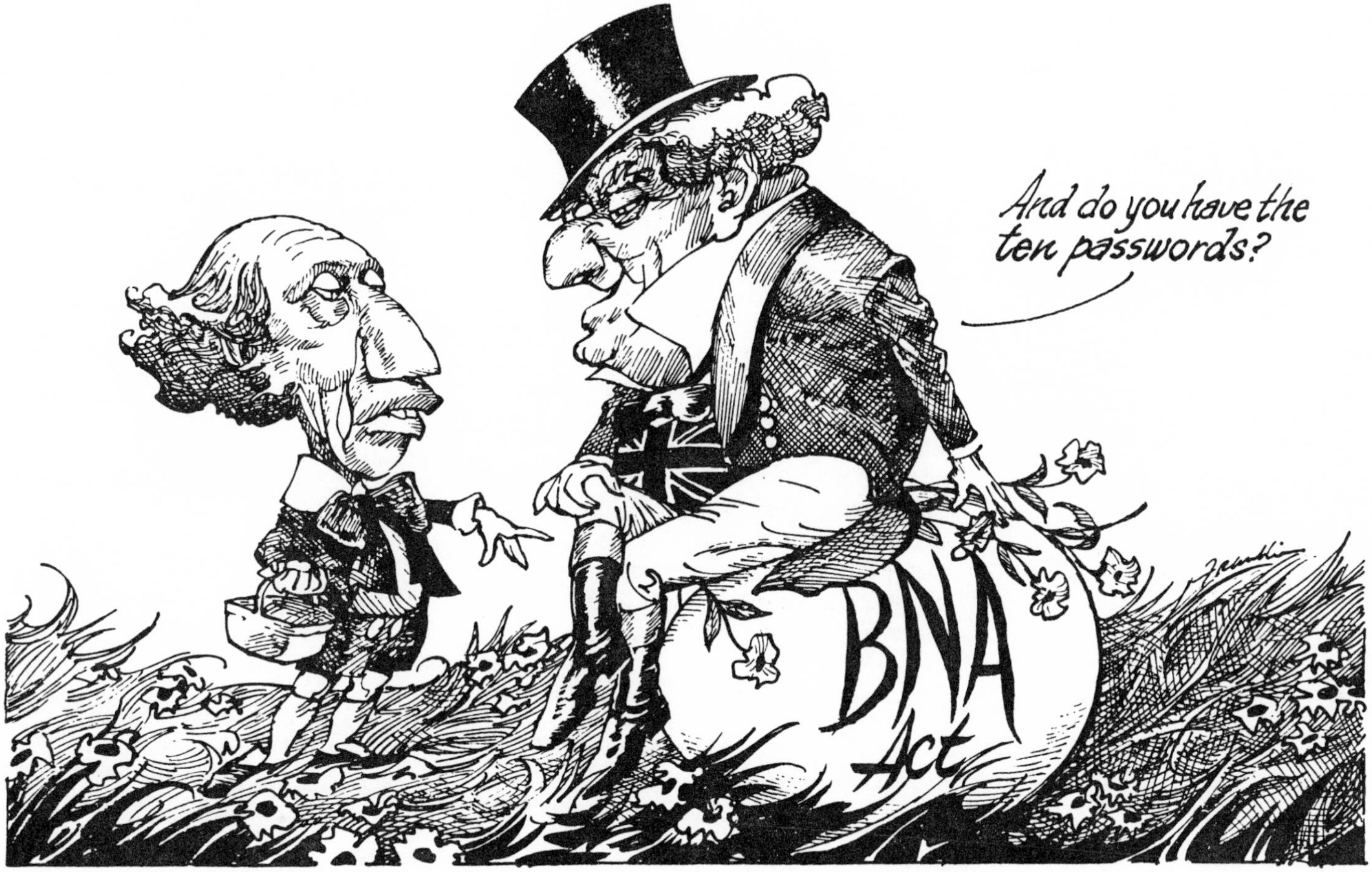
And do you have the
ten passwords?
BNA
Act

"Let us grant him this — when he presided over the patriation of the new constitution in the spring of 1982, Trudeau completed the grand task which had brought him into federal politics nearly seventeen years earlier, and into which he had dragged--at times almost willy nilly--the entire Canadian nation...Trudeau had established a federal framework which aspired to protect the basic rights of all Canadians, and to give French Canadians in particular a plausible alternative to the dubious benefits of separation."

—Charles Taylor
Radical Tories

FRANK EDWARDS
THE WHIG-STANDARD, APRIL 21, 1982

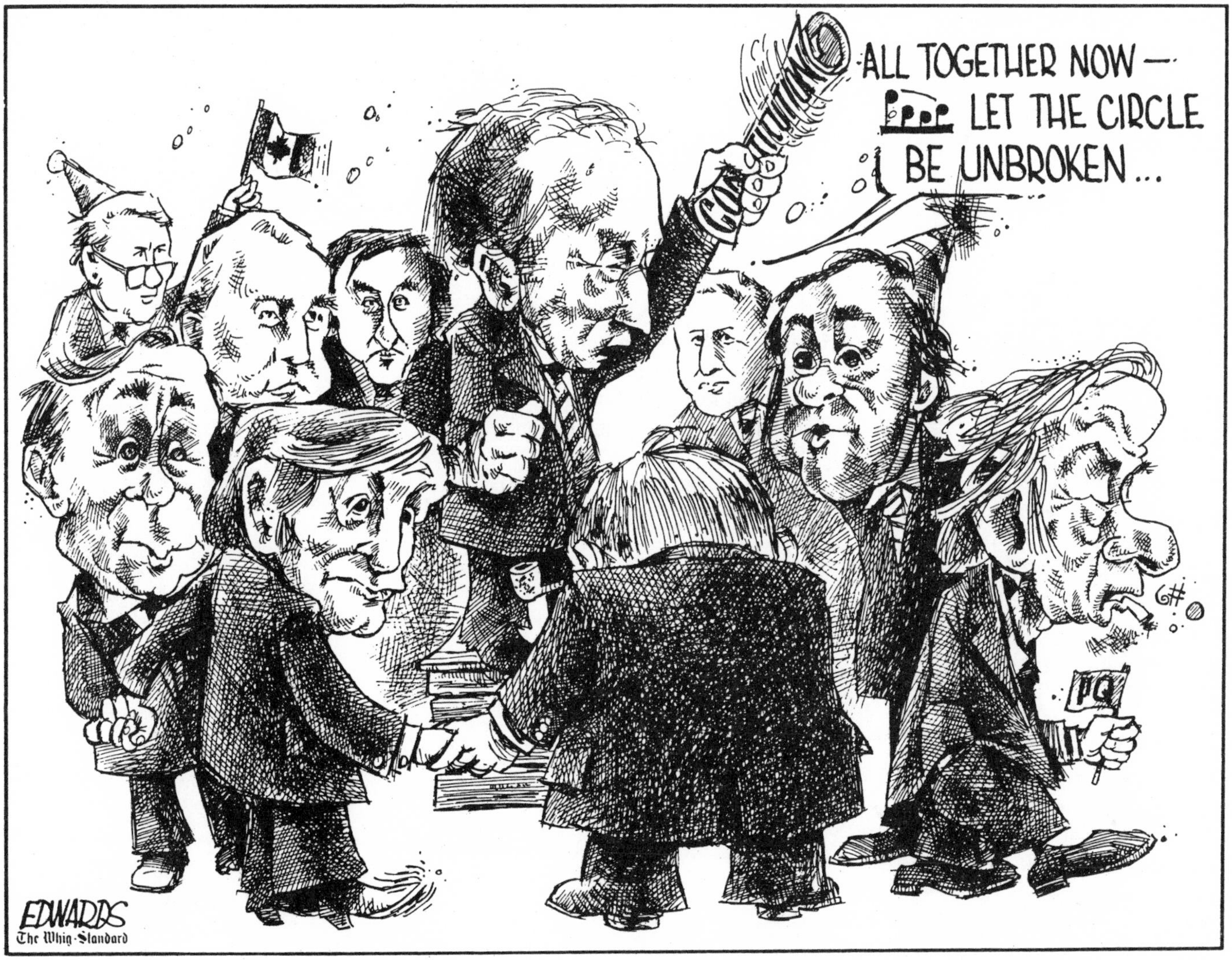
CONSTITUTION
ALL TOGETHER NOW —
LET THE CIRCLE
BE UNBROKEN ...
PQ
EDWARDS
The Whig-Standard

"Though Canadians are baffled by the turgid complexity of the Constitution, they began to realize that reforming the British North America Act was the only way to put the country back together."

—June Callwood
Portrait of Canada

ROY PETERSON
VANCOUVER SUN, OCTOBER 28, 1981

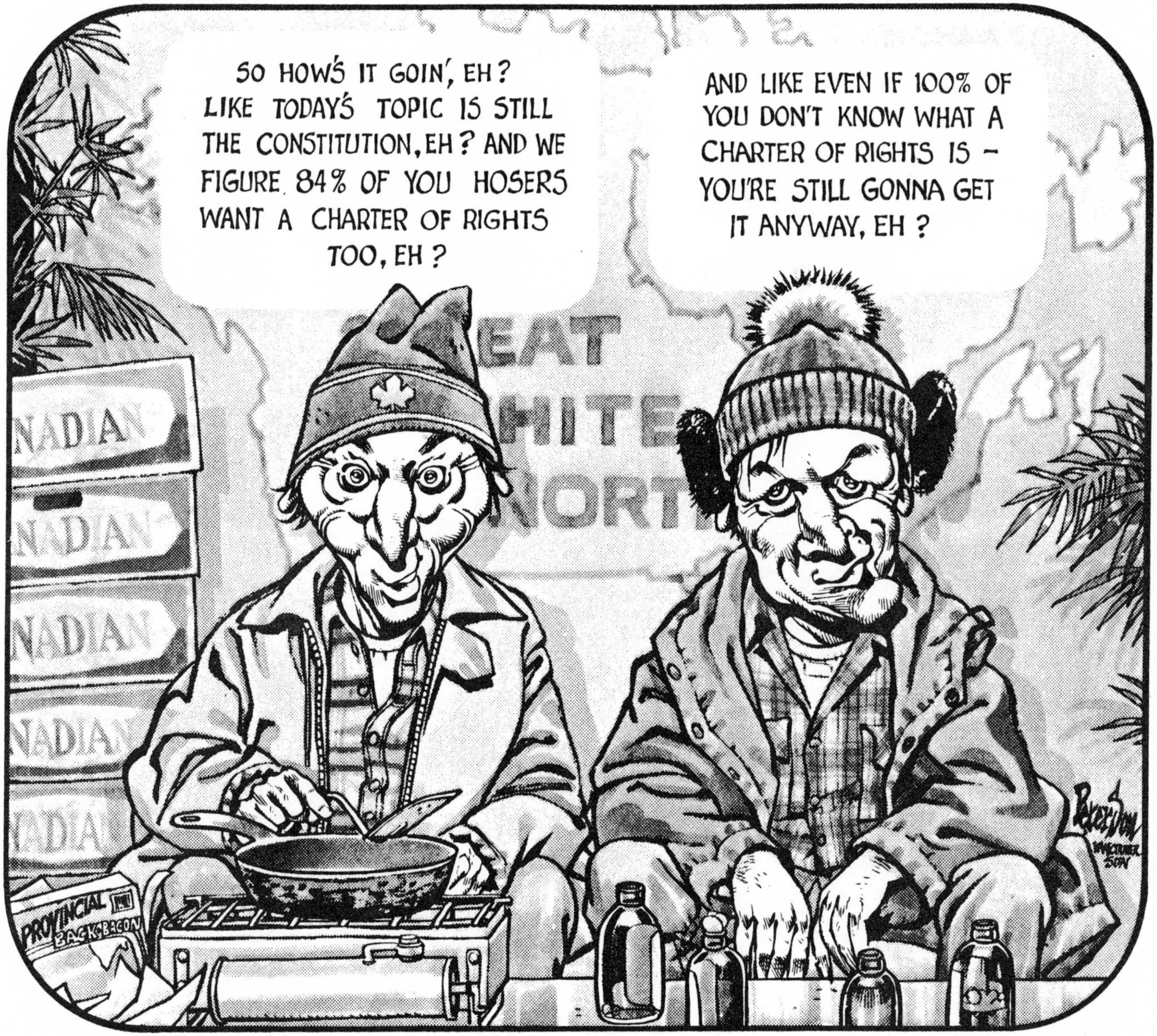
SO HOW'S IT GOIN', EH? LIKE TODAY'S TOPIC IS STILL THE CONSTITUTION, EH? AND WE FIGURE 84% OF YOU HOSERS WANT A CHARTER OF RIGHTS TOO, EH?
AND LIKE EVEN IF 100% OF YOU DON'T KNOW WHAT A CHARTER OF RIGHTS IS – YOU'RE STILL GONNA GET IT ANYWAY, EH?

The MacPatriation Brothers

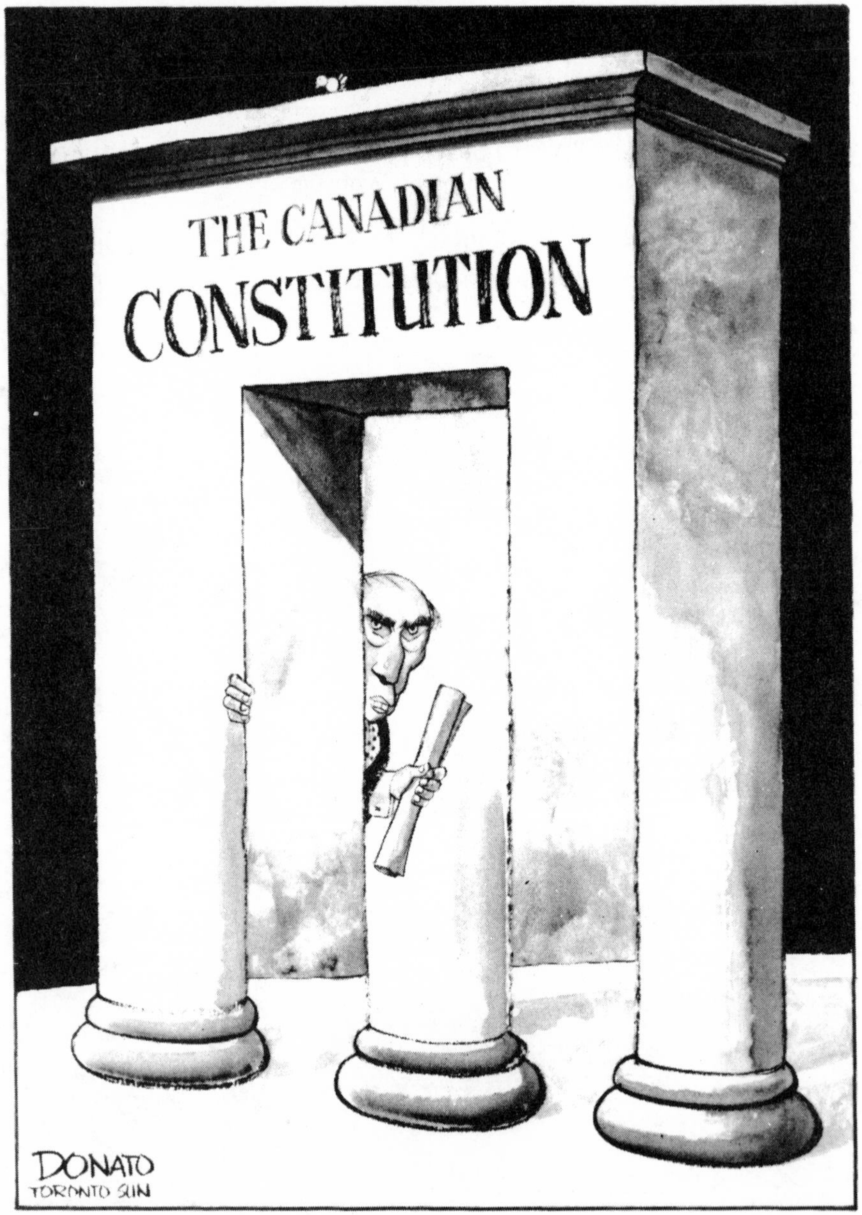
THE CANADIAN
CONSTITUTION
DONATO
TORONTO SUN

ANDY DONATO
THE TORONTO SUN, JANUARY 27, 1981

The Architect

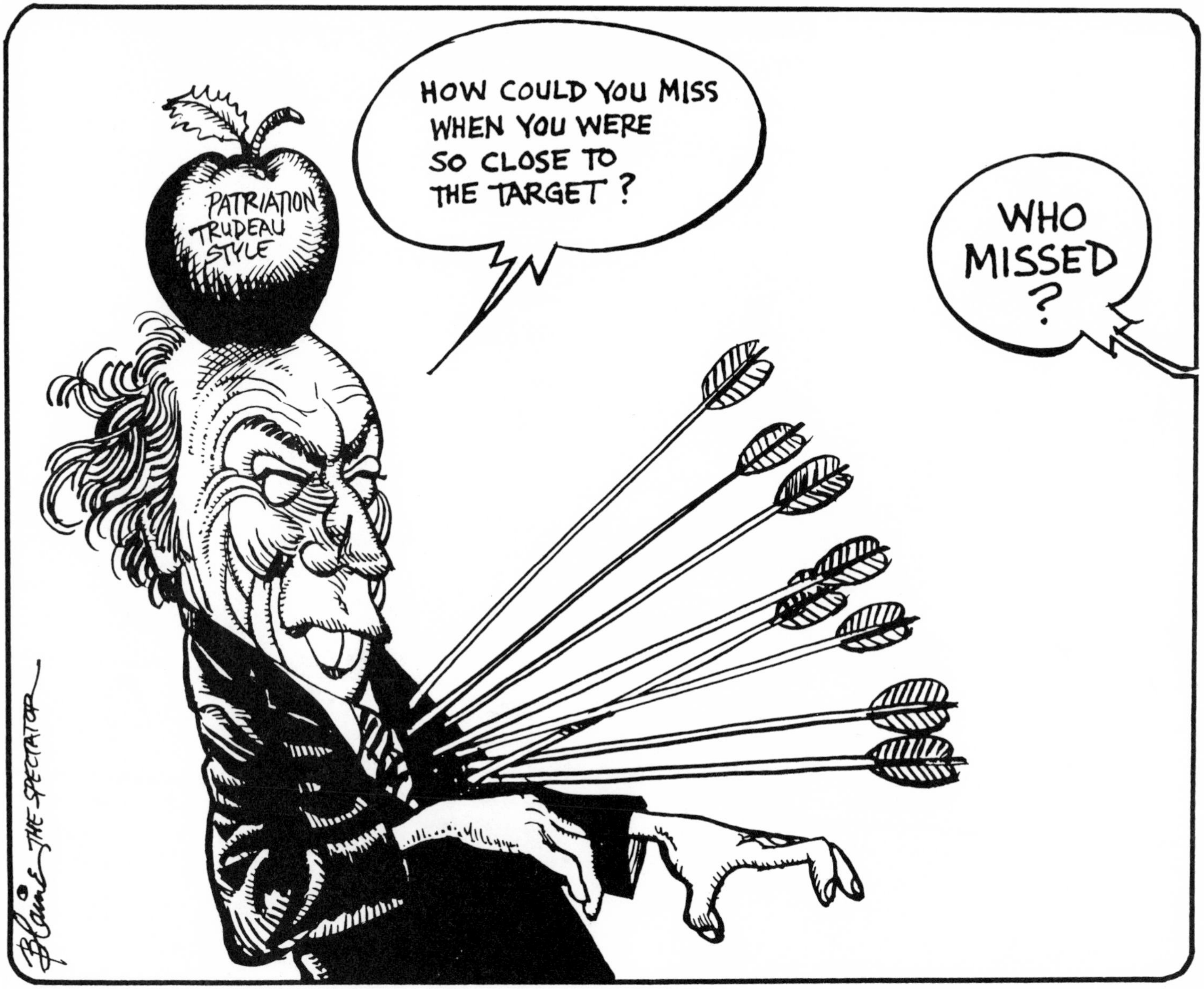
HOW COULD YOU MISS WHEN YOU WERE SO CLOSE TO THE TARGET ?
PATRIATION TRUDEAU STYLE
WHO MISSED ?
Blaine THE SPECTATOR

BLAINE
THE HAMILTON SPECTATOR, SEPTEMBER 24, 1980

"La raison avant la passion, reason before passion."

—Pierre Elliott Trudeau
Personal maxim

EDD ULUSCHAK
EDMONTON JOURNAL

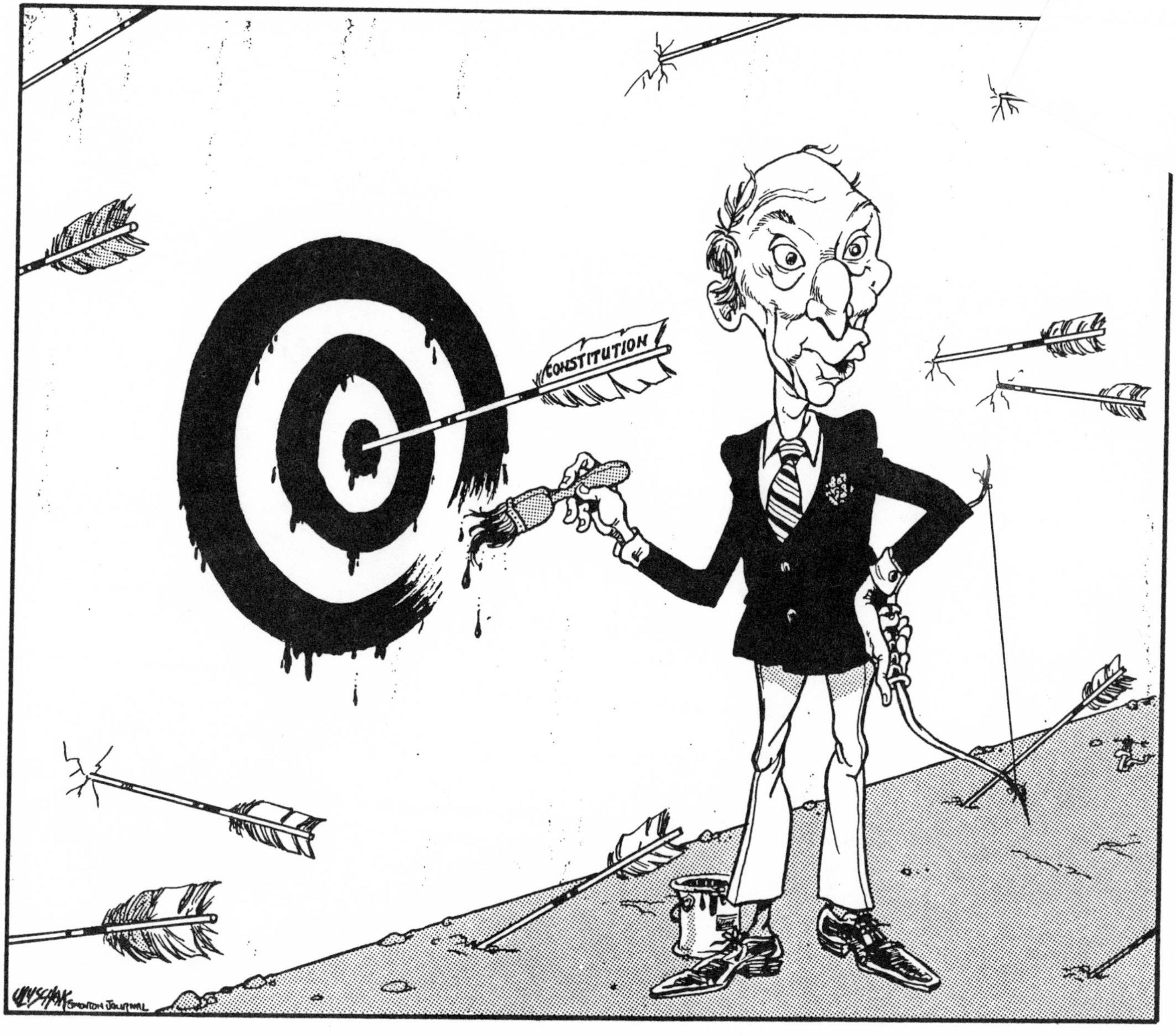
CONSTITUTION

"That wasn't so hard, was it, fellas?"

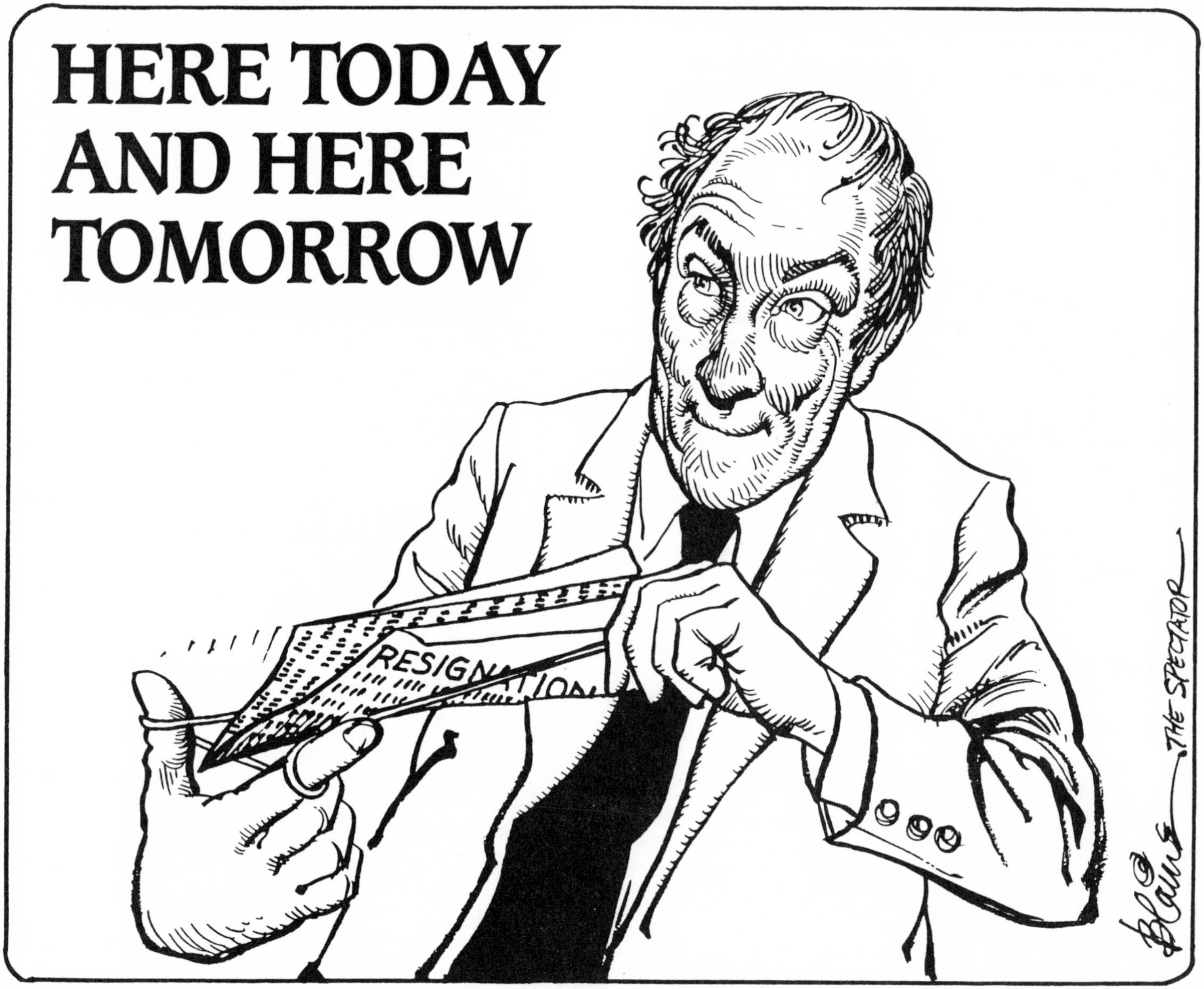
HERE TODAY AND HERE TOMORROW
THE SPECTATOR
Blaine

BLAINE
THE HAMILTON SPECTATOR

“**He chose February** 29 to announce his resignation so that the Conservatives could celebrate only once every four years.”

—Anon.

BLAINE
THE HAMILTON SPECTATOR, MARCH 6, 1984

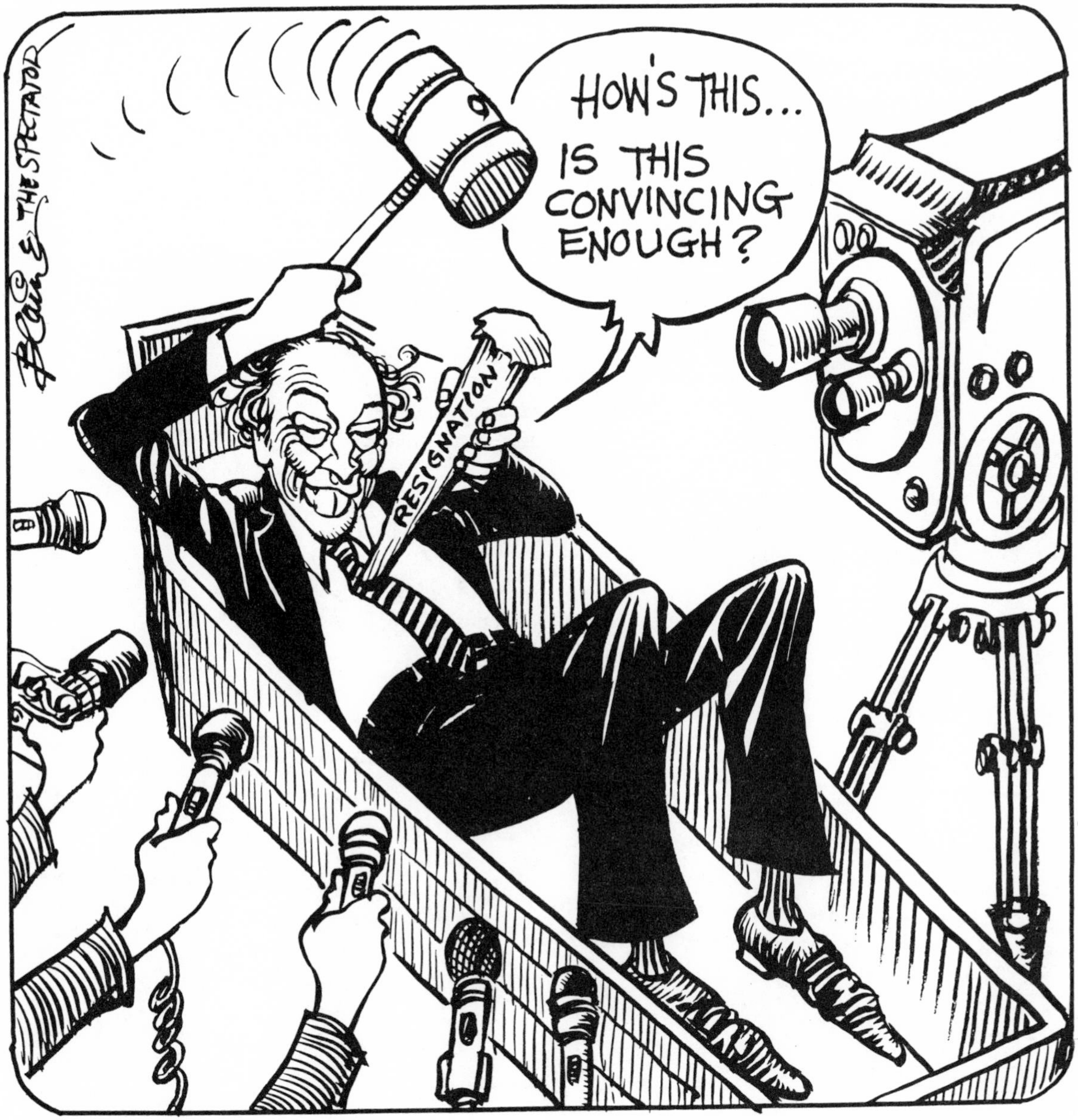
HOW'S THIS...
IS THIS CONVINCING ENOUGH?
RESIGNATION
THE SPECTATOR

"It was not the magnitude of Trudeau's failure (to unite the country) that produced this rage against him in English-speaking Canada — indeed, their animus was the nearest thing we had to shared opinion — but rather it was what they remembered of their expectations of him, which were not less than the children of Israel had expected of Moses."

—Dalton Camp
Points of Departure

EDD ULUSCHAK
EDMONTON JOURNAL, SEPTEMBER 16, 1983

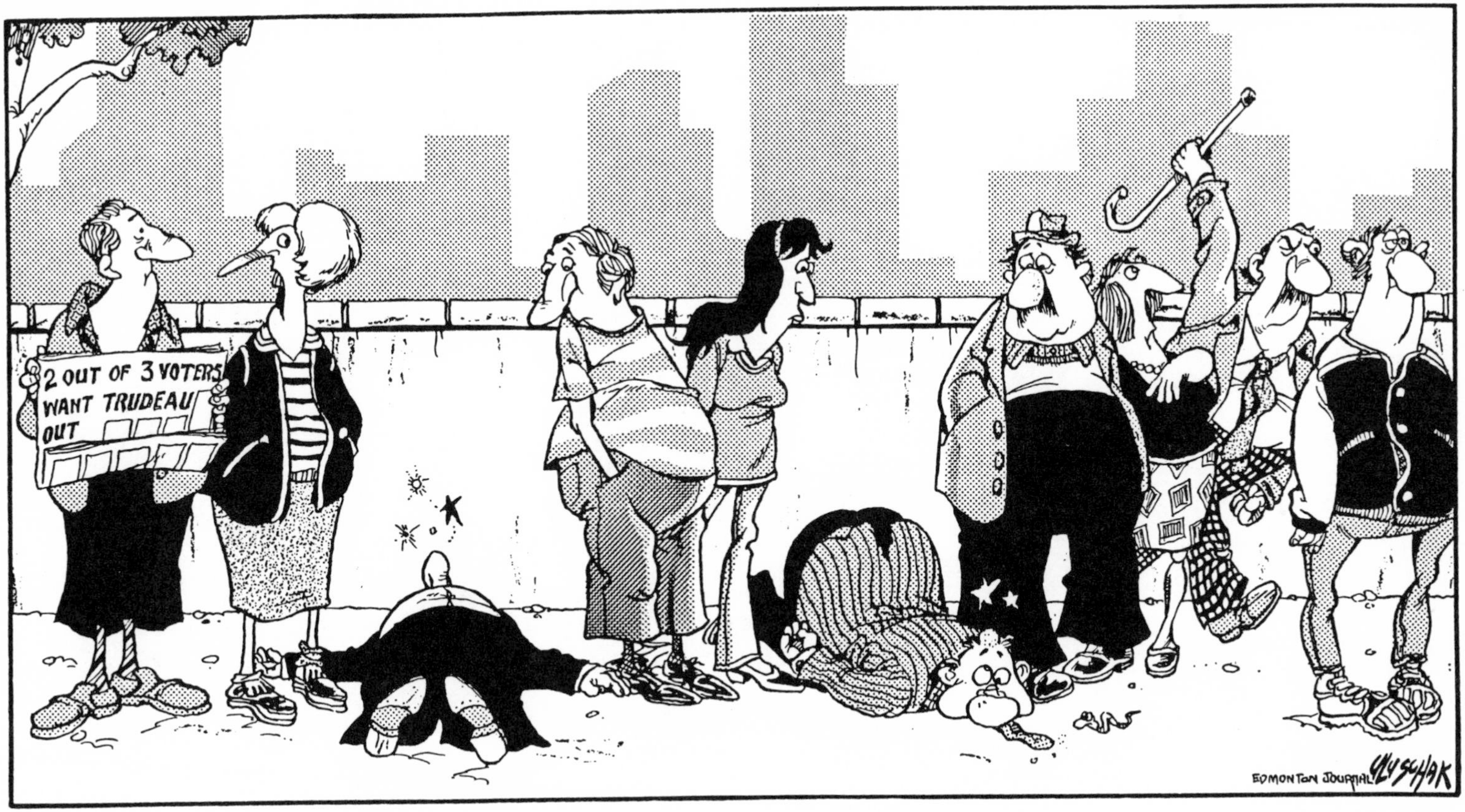
2 OUT OF 3 VOTERS WANT TRUDEAU OUT
EDMONTON JOURNAL
UYUSCHAK

"Eustice is incensed at every third person for actually wanting Trudeau to stay."

"The things I will do after I retire?

"Many books I still want to read. Perhaps learn to play the piano better. See the few remaining countries that I've never visited. See my children grow up and begin to fulfil themselves. Those are the things that are still ahead."

—Pierre Elliott Trudeau,
interview with David Frost
February, 1982

EDD ULUSCHAK
EDMONTON JOURNAL, NOVEMBER 27, 1981

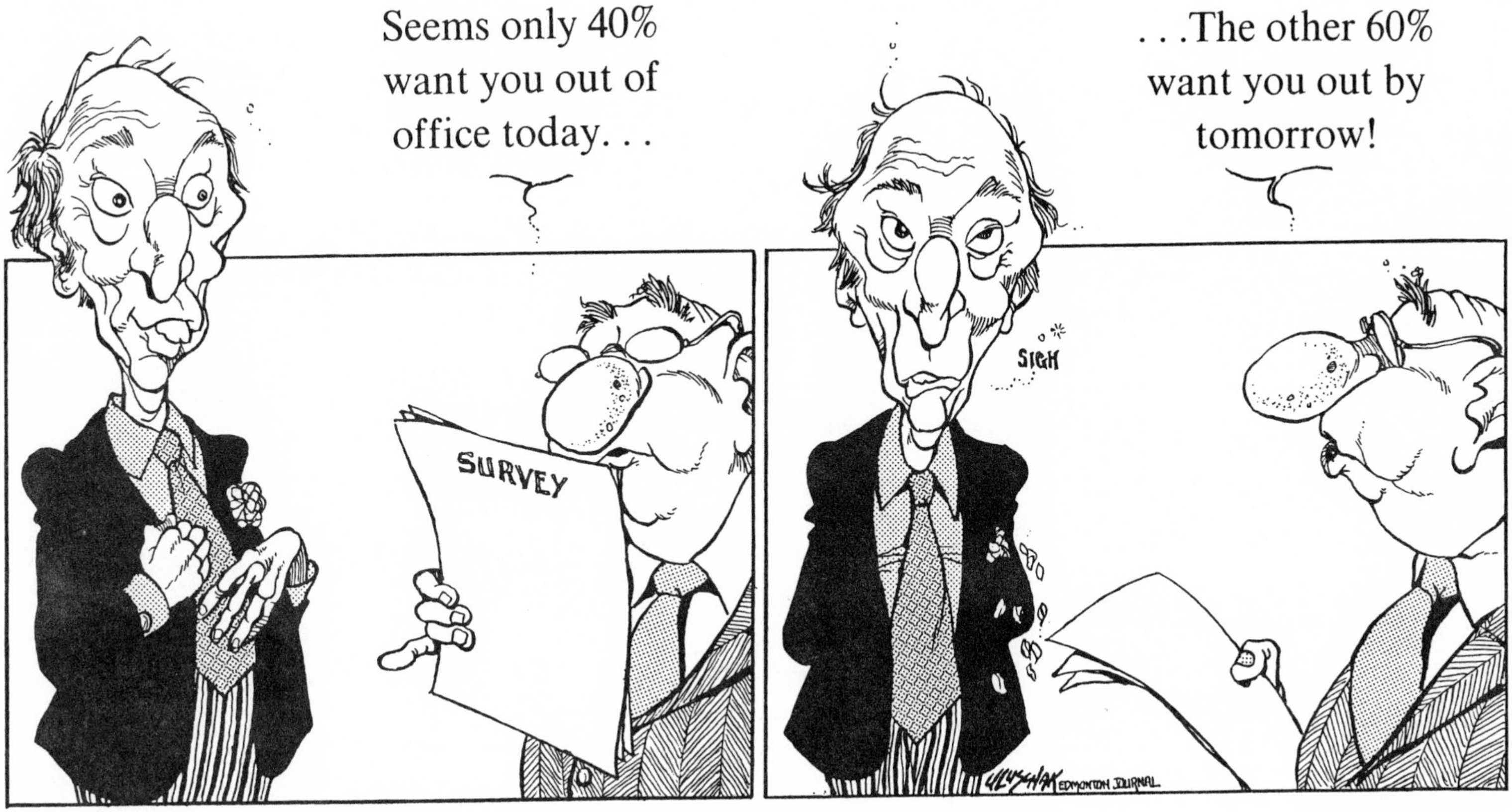
Seems only 40% want you out of office today. . .
SURVEY
. . .The other 60% want you out by tomorrow!
SIGH
EDMONTON JOURNAL

"I used to be all in favor of Canada. Some of my best friends, and all that. But that was up until they elected that Commie Prime Minister. Trudeau is his name. A Commie, everybody knows it. A fellow from out west, he got up in the Congress and said it right out, that the Prime Minister of Canada was a Commie. Well, I naturally expected that to be the end of Mr. Trudeau. No such thing. If they didn't go and put him right back in the next time. All I can say is that was the end of Canada, as far as I'm concerned, and I don't care who knows it."

—A farmer, near Rutland, Vermont
from As They See Us *by Walter Stewart*

BLAINE
THE HAMILTON SPECTATOR, MARCH 3, 1983

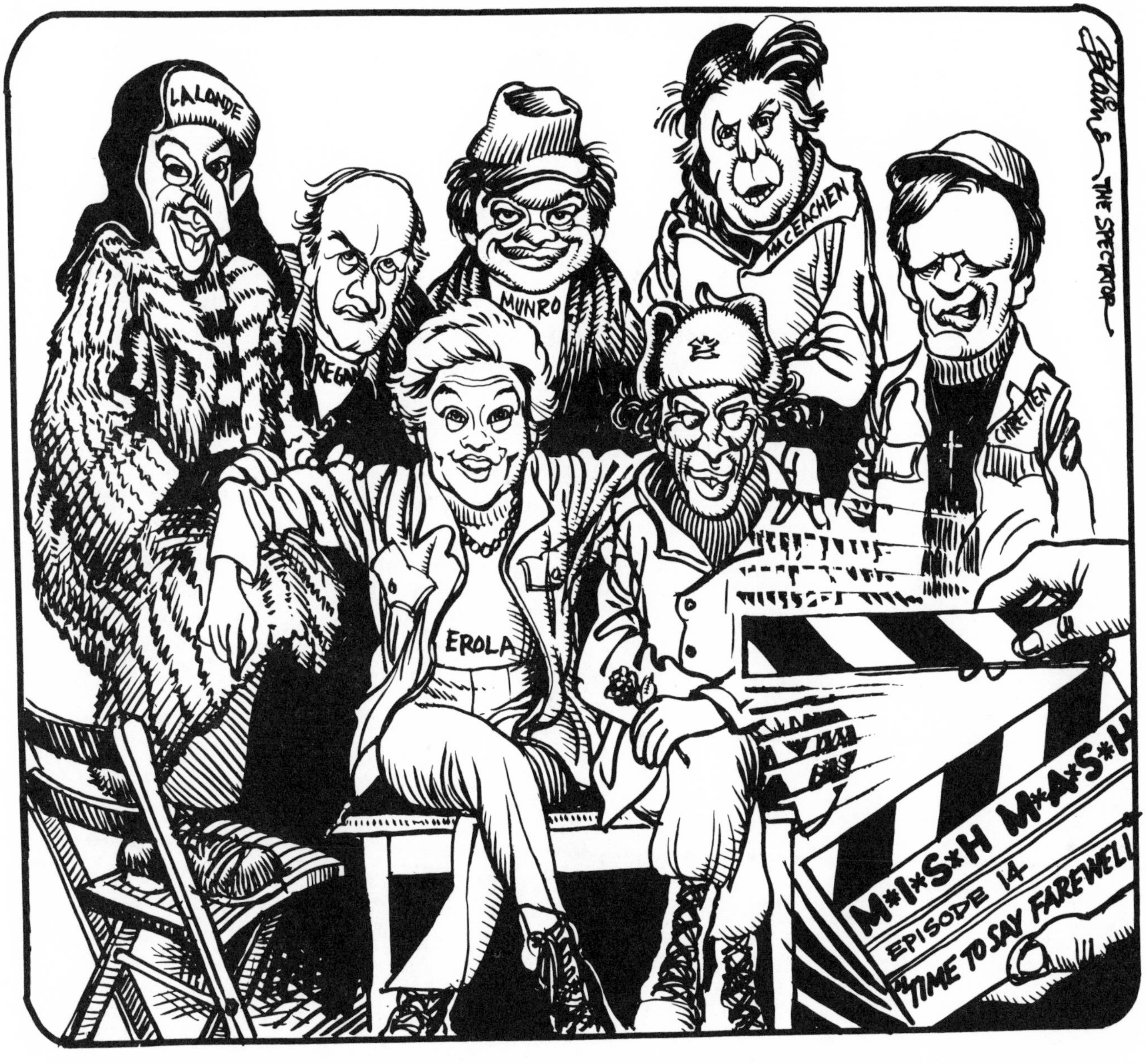
THE SPECTATOR
LALONDE
MUNRO
MACEACHEN
CHRETIEN
EROLA
M*I*S*H M*A*S*H
EPISODE 14
"TIME TO SAY FAREWELL"

"There is no easy way or ideal time to leave. There are always strong public and private reasons, both for going and for staying on. At a point in time one simply makes the decision as to what is best."

—Pierre Elliott Trudeau
November 21, 1979

DUNCAN MACPHERSON
THE TORONTO STAR, NOVEMBER, 1979

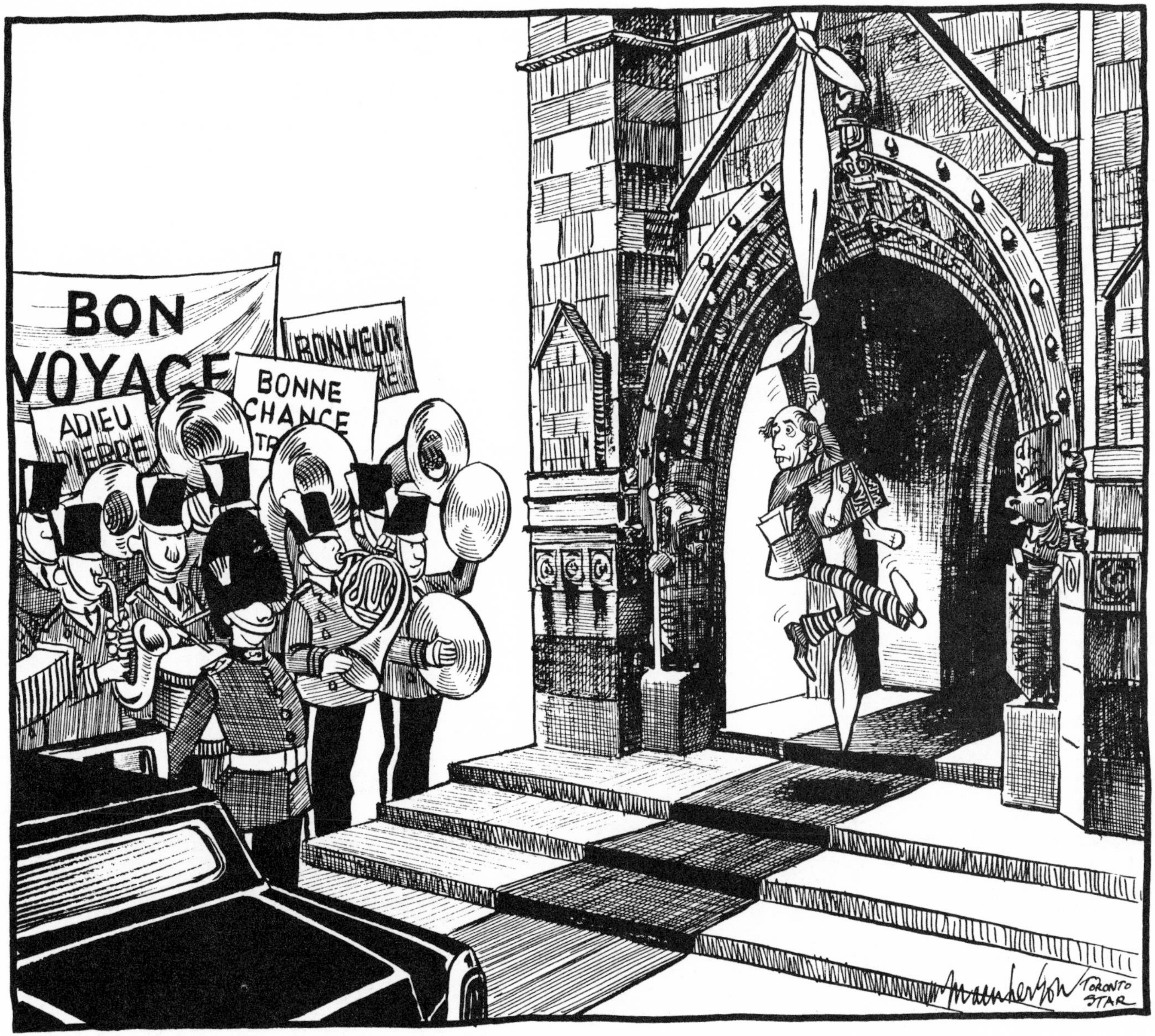
BON VOYAGE
BONHEUR
BONNE CHANCE
ADIEU
TORONTO STAR

"To be frank— yes, I'm sorry. He sure made things more interesting— not necessarily more appealing, but more interesting."
—*René Levesque on hearing of Trudeau's final resignation*

FRANKLIN
THE GLOBE AND MAIL, MAY 2, 1984

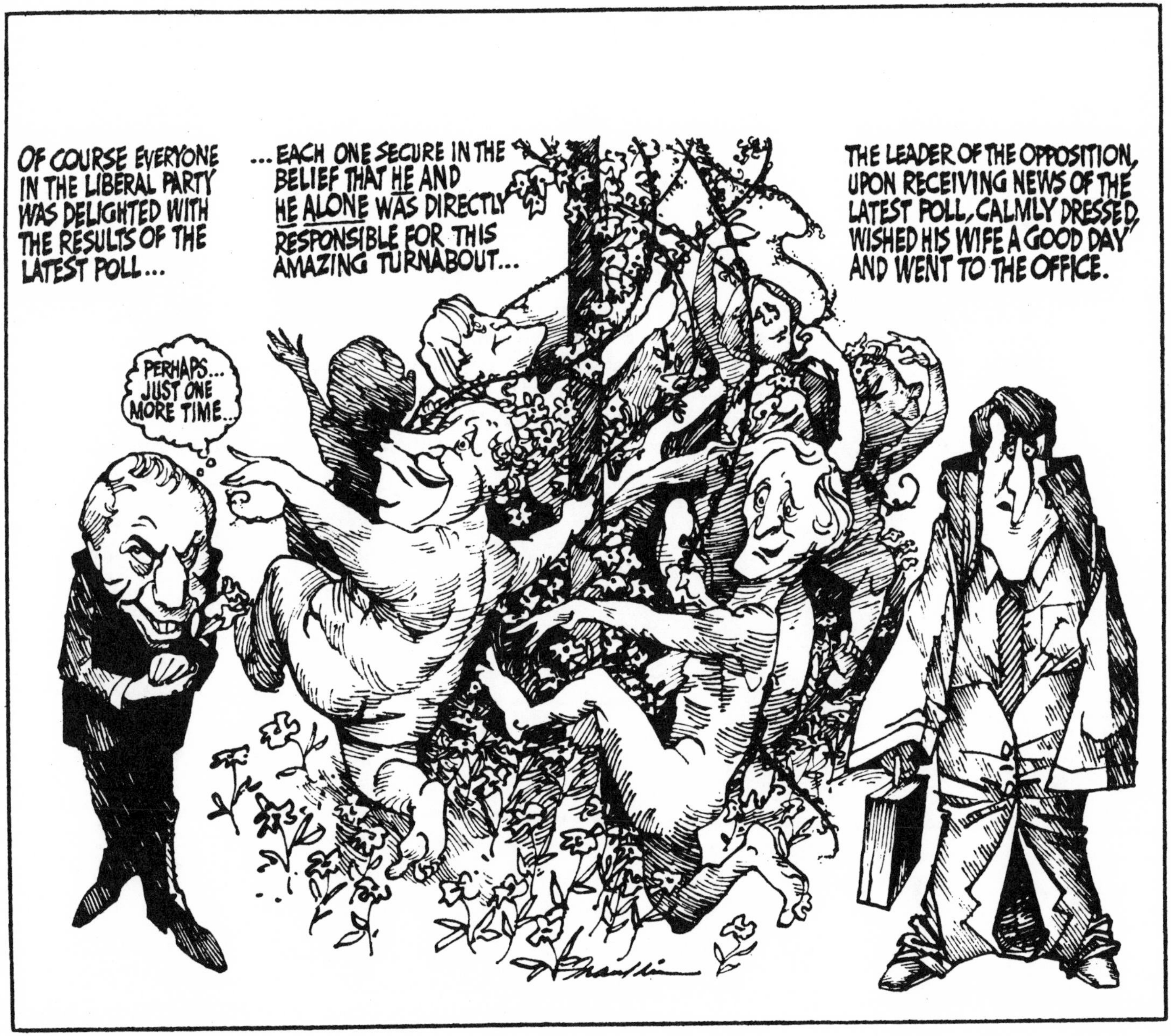
OF COURSE EVERYONE IN THE LIBERAL PARTY WAS DELIGHTED WITH THE RESULTS OF THE LATEST POLL...
...EACH ONE SECURE IN THE BELIEF THAT HE AND HE ALONE WAS DIRECTLY RESPONSIBLE FOR THIS AMAZING TURNABOUT...
THE LEADER OF THE OPPOSITION, UPON RECEIVING NEWS OF THE LATEST POLL, CALMLY DRESSED, WISHED HIS WIFE A GOOD DAY AND WENT TO THE OFFICE.
PERHAPS... JUST ONE MORE TIME...

"I had a good day yesterday, worked on aboriginal rights, and it seemed like a good day to have a last day. ... I had a good day. It was a great walk in the snow. I went to judo, felt very combative, and here I am."

—Pierre Elliott Trudeau
February 29, 1984

"I wish to inform you of my decision to resign from the leadership of the Liberal Party. The experience of being Leader of our great party has been one of the joys of my life but I now feel this is the appropriate time for someone else to assume this challenge.

"I want to thank each and every member of the Liberal Party for the support, loyalty and friendship I have enjoyed. I will always be deeply grateful to the Liberal Party for giving me the opportunity to serve my country."

—Pierre Elliott Trudeau
in a letter to Iona Campagnolo
President of the Liberal Party of Canada
February 29, 1984

AISLIN
MONTREAL GAZETTE, NOVEMBER 26, 1979

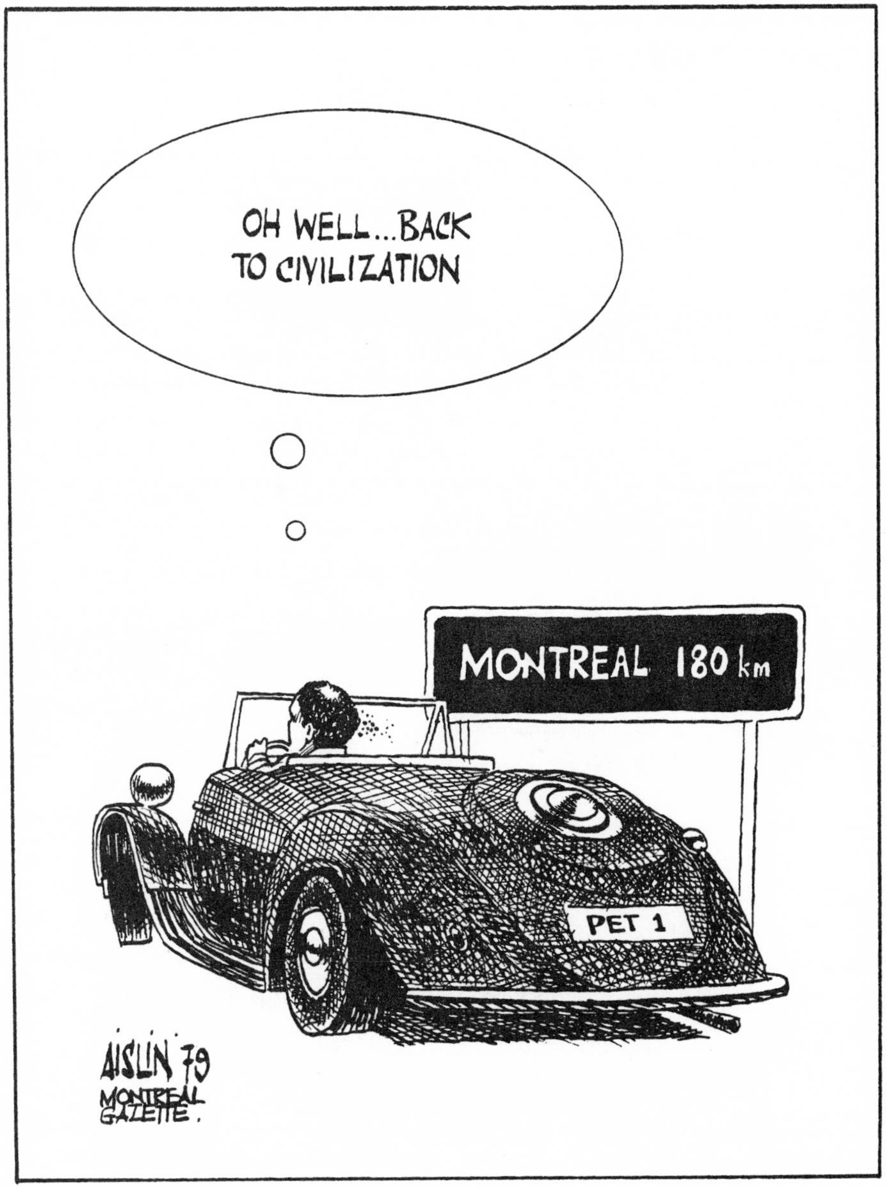
OH WELL...BACK TO CIVILIZATION
MONTREAL 180 km
PET 1
AISLIN '79
MONTREAL GAZETTE.

BIBLIOGRAPHY OF SOURCES

Bom, Philip C. *Trudeau's Canada.* St. Catherines: Guardian Publishing, 1977.

Callwood, June. *Portrait of Canada.* Toronto: Doubleday Canada, 1981.

Camp, Dalton. *An Eclectic Eel.* Ottawa: Deneau Publishers, 1981.

Camp, Dalton. *Points of Departure.* Ottawa: Deneau and Greenberg, 1974.

Columbo, John Robert. *Columbo's Canadian Quotations.* Edmonton: Hurtig Publishers, 1974.

Desbarats, Peter. *Canada Lost, Canada Found.* Toronto: McClelland and Stewart, 1981.

Desbarats, Peter. *Rene: A Canadian in Search of a Country.* Toronto: McClelland and Stewart, 1976.

Fotheringham, Allan. *Malice in Blunderland: Or How the Grits Stole Christmas.* Toronto: Key Porter Books, 1982.

Gwyn, Richard. *The Northern Magus: Pierre Trudeau and Canadians.* Toronto: McClelland and Stewart, 1980.

Haggart, Ron, and Golden, Aubrey E. *Rumours of War.* Toronto: James Lorimer and Company, 1979.

Hockin, Thomas A. *The Prime Minister and Political Leadership in Canada.* Toronto: Prentice-Hall, 1971.

Laxer, James, and Laxer, Robert. *The Liberal Idea of Canada: Pierre Trudeau and the Question of Canada's Survival.* Toronto: James Lorimer and Company, 1977.

Martin, Lawrence. *The Presidents and the Prime Ministers.* Toronto: Doubleday Canada, 1982.

Martin, Paul. *A Very Private Life.* Ottawa: Deneau Publishers, 1983.

Munro, John, and Inglis, Alex, eds. *Mike: The Memoirs of the Right Honourable Lester B. Pearson.* Toronto: The University of Toronto Press, 1975.

Newman, Peter C. *Distemper of Our Times.* Toronto: McClelland and Stewart, 1968.

Newman, Peter C. *Home Country.* Toronto: McClelland and Stewart, 1973.

Newman, Christina McCall. *Grits: An Intimate Portrait of the Liberal Party.* Toronto: Macmillan of Canada, 1982.

Penniman, Howerd R., ed. *Canada at the Polls: The General Election of 1974.* Washington, D.C.: American Institute for Public Policy Research, 1975.

Porter, Anna, and Harris, Marjorie, eds. *Farewell to the 70s.* Toronto: Thomas Nelson and Sons, 1979.

Radwanski, George. *Trudeau.* Toronto: Macmillan of Canada, 1978.

Shackleton, Doris French. *Tommy Douglas.* Toronto: McClelland and Stewart, 1975.

Simpson, Jeffrey. *Discipline of Power.* Toronto: Personal Library Publishers, 1980.

Stewart, Walter. *As They See Us.* Toronto: McClelland and Stewart, 1977.

Stewart, Walter. *Shrug: Trudeau in Power.* Toronto: New Press, 1971.

Stursberg, Peter. *Lester Pearson and the Dream of Unity.* Toronto: Doubleday Canada, 1978.

Taylor, Charles. *Radical Tories.* Toronto: House of Anansi, 1982.

Trudeau, Pierre Elliott. *Federalism and the French Canadians.* Toronto: Macmillan of Canada, 1968.

Trudeau, Pierre Elliott, and Hebert, Jacques. *Two Innocents in Red China.* Translated by I.M. Owen. Toronto: Oxford University Press, 1970.

INDEX OF CARTOONISTS

AISLIN (Terry Mosher)/*The Gazette,* Montreal
57, 89, 93, 97, 99, 157
BLAINE/*The Spectator,* Hamilton
Cover, 45, 100, 139, 143, 145, 151
DONATO, Andy/*The Toronto Sun*
51, 65, 66, 72, 91, 101, 138
EDWARDS, Frank/*The Whig-Standard,* Kingston, Ontario
69, 85, 119, 123, 135
FRANKLIN, Ed/*The Globe and Mail,* Toronto
19, 37, 39, 49, 63, 75, 76, 77, 87, 113, 133, 155
GRASTON, Mike/*The Windsor Star*
55, 83, 103, 105
LARTER, John/*The Toronto Star*
82
MACPHERSON, Duncan/*The Toronto Star*
13, 15, 17, 23, 25, 29, 31, 33, 107, 109, 111, 131, 153
PETERSON, Roy/*The Vancouver Sun*
70, 73, 137
RAESIDE, Adrian/*The Times-Colonist,* Victoria
41, 53, 67, 71, 79, 115, 117, 129
REIDFORD, James G./*The Globe and Mail,* Toronto
21, 27, 43, 47, 68
TING (Merle Tingley)/*The London Free Press*
35, 160
ULUSCHAK, Edd/*The Edmonton Journal*
59, 61, 81, 95, 121, 125, 127, 141, 147, 149

A TEAR-STAINED REGRET

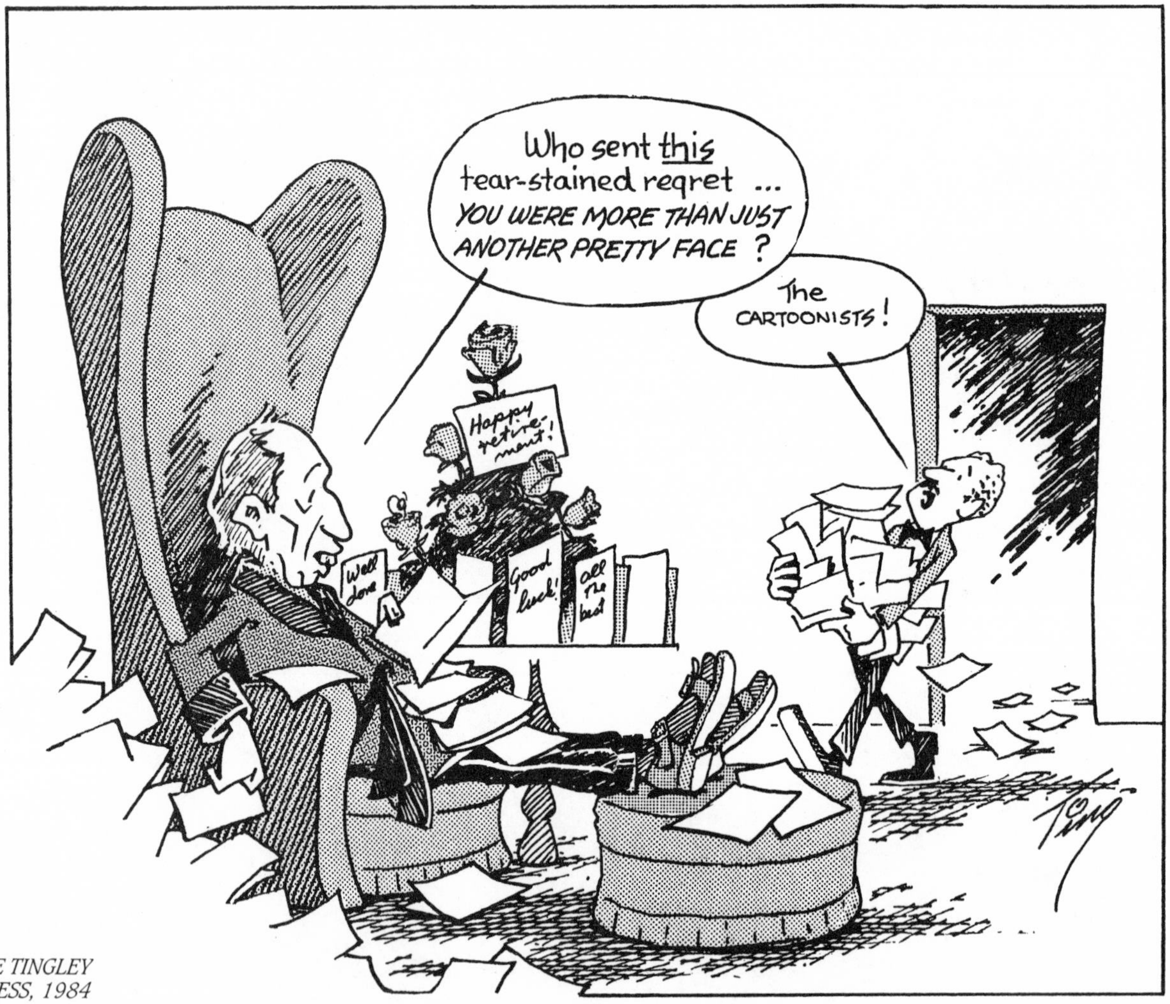

Who sent this tear-stained regret ... YOU WERE MORE THAN JUST ANOTHER PRETTY FACE ?
The CARTOONISTS!
Happy retire-ment!
Well done
Good luck!
All the best

MERLE TINGLEY
LONDON FREE PRESS, 1984